Caring for your
DOG

HELEN DIGBY

magnet™
& steel

© 2014 Magnet & Steel Ltd

This edition published by Magnet & Steel Ltd

Printed 2014

This book is distributed in the UK by
Magnet & Steel Ltd
Unit 6,
Vale Business Park
Cowbridge
CF71 7PF

sales@magnetsteel.com

ISBN: 978-1-907337-74-1

DS0178. Caring for Your Dog

Creative Director: Sarah King
Project editor: Anna Southgate
Designer: Jade Sienkiewicz
Photography: Paul Forrester

Printed in Korea

Material from this book previously appeared in *The Dog Care Handbook*

1 3 5 7 9 10 8 6 4 2

Caring for your
DOG

contents

ONE

introduction

"Ah! You should keep dogs – fine animals – sagacious creatures ..." as Mr. Winkle advised Mr. Pickwick in Charles Dickens' *The Pickwick Papers*, and it is a piece of advice that has been followed by millions of us for centuries. It is a cliché to remark that a dog is man's best friend, but it is a statement that has been reinforced over thousands of years. Human beings and dogs share a symbiotic relationship in many ways: people adopt dogs as pets and care for them in return for companionship, protection, and unquestioning devotion. Man and dog have evolved a unique, inseparable partnership over the centuries. Owning a dog is a privilege and a responsibility, but canine devotion must be repaid with practical care, security, and respect. Dogs have provided humans with support and protection – both physical and psychological – for thousands of years, and the least that the human race can do after such a long relationship is to ensure that their domestic animals are happy and fulfilled.

LARGE AND IMMENSELY STRONG, SAINT BERNARDS REQUIRE LOTS OF SPACE.

INTRODUCE YOUR DOG TO OTHER PETS GRADUALLY.

SENSITIVE AND GENTLE, LABRADORS ARE POPULAR FAMILY PETS.

THE BLOODHOUND'S LONG MUZZLE AND PENDULOUS EARS GIVE IT A DOLOROUS APPEARANCE.

There are more than four hundred distinct breeds of dog, and their diverse appearances are entirely the result of human intervention. Dogs have been bred to suit the whims of their owners, and the variety of their looks is reflected in their many talents and characters. The steady Saint Bernard, which exudes calm, has been trained as a mountain-rescue animal; the exceptional sense of smell of bloodhounds, Labrador retrievers and German shepherd dogs is utilized by law-enforcement agencies to uncover drugs; while innumerable breeds make wonderful companions, providing their owners with unlimited affection and devotion. Dogs are one of the two most popular domestic animals in the world – the other is the cat.

Most humans have a basic instinct to care for living things and, for many people, dogs fulfill this need. Dogs are pack animals and will obey the person whom they regard as their pack leader – usually their owner. They are essentially uncomplicated animals, grateful for a warm home, regular supply of food, and a small amount of territory to defend. They are unquestioningly loyal, fiercely protective, and do not criticize us – few humans are so amenable!

Owning a happy and healthy dog is a rewarding occupation, but this can only be achieved through proper care. This book provides a comprehensive introduction to caring for dogs; it attempts to explain

THE SAINT BERNARD AND THE CHIHUAHUA OCCUPY OPPOSITE
ENDS OF THE CANINE SPECTRUM IN TERMS OF SIZE.

certain aspects of doggy behaviour and provides details of how to keep your dog in the best-possible health. It also offers some solutions for common problems that can occur, even in the best-regulated kennels.

THE ORIGIN OF THE SPECIES

Although a brief review of the dog's ancient forebears may not seem entirely relevant to a twenty-first-century book on dog care, careful study of the dog's evolution provides answers to many aspects of canine behaviour.

No animal family on Earth, wild or domestic, is as varied as that of the dog. Sizes range from the 154 lb (70 kg) Saint Bernard to the 5.5 lb (2.5 kg) Chihuahua; looks are as diverse as the shaggy, dreadlocked komondor or the completely hairless Xoloizcuintle; the Irish wolfhound has exceptionally long legs, whereas, at the other end of the spectrum, the dachshund's short legs barely raise its body off the ground.

The dog family, *Canidae*, contains about thirty-five species grouped into fourteen genera. They include the domestic dog (*Canis familiaris*), the wolf (*Canis lupus*), fourteen species of fox, and four species of jackal. They are native to almost every part of the world and clearly belong to an adaptable family, living across a diversity of habitats, from tropical rainforests to frozen northern woods, from deserts to icy tundra.

Fossil evidence suggests that dogs evolved from a small, weasel-like mammal called Miacis that lived about 60 million years ago. The first canids, the Cynodictis, evolved from Miacis and appeared during the Miocene Era, between thirty and forty million

GERMAN SHEPHERDS ARE THE MOST NUMEROUS BREED IN THE WORLD.

MAN'S BEST FRIEND HAS BEEN IMMORTALIZED IN ART FOR CENTURIES.

years ago; they were medium-sized animals, longer than they were tall, with a long tail and fairly thick coat. Two branches descended from Cynodictis, Cynodesmus in Africa and Tomarctus in Eurasia, the ancestor of wolves, dogs, and foxes.

It is hard to believe that such diverse animals are descended from a single common ancestor. Charles Darwin was so overwhelmed by the sheer number of different dog breeds that he propounded the theory of mixed descent from two wild species, the wolf (*Canis lupus*) and the golden jackal (*Canis aureus*). Over recent years, experts have agreed that the domestic dog is probably descended from the wolf: its bone structure, especially that of the skull and teeth, is nearly identical to small wolves, and its behavioural patterns reinforce this evidence. One study recorded ninety different behavioural traits in domestic dogs, and all except for nineteen minor characteristics were shared by wolves. By contrast, the behavioural patterns observed in wolves that were not shared by dogs related to hunting in situations rarely encountered by domestic dogs. When dogs have mated with wolves, they have usually produced fertile offspring, which suggests very strongly that dogs and wolves are part of the same family.

It is likely that wolves were first domesticated during the Stone Age or, more properly, Paleolithic times, approximately fourteen thousand years ago.

Archeological remains of canine jawbone fragments show that Palaeolithic dogs had a short jaw compared to the wolf, which probably evolved as a result of changes in diet. Human beings lived by hunting and foraging for food every day, and, having observed the hunting techniques of wolves, may have decided to befriend them with a view to utilizing their skills. It is more likely, however, that the relationship between man and wolf, and subsequently dog, was accidental. Wolf cubs may have been adopted as pets – Palaeolithic people were probably as susceptible as their modern descendants to small, cuddly, furry animals. Like dogs, wolf cubs can be trained if they are adopted by humans at around three to seven weeks of age, and demonstrate as much affection as dogs towards their human masters.

Palaeolithic wolves and humans shared a number of common habits. Both were primarily active during the daytime, hunting and foraging. Wolves are intelligent creatures that are emotionally responsive and able to convey a wide array of nonverbal messages through changes in posture, attitude, and facial expression. A great deal of human communication is similarly nonverbal, so it is possible that Palaeolithic people built a cooperative relationship with their adopted wolves. Both humans and wolves live in "packs." Palaeolithic man inhabited a social group of family members numbering approximately ten to twenty individuals, who

DOGS AND WOLVES SHARE MANY
BEHAVIOURAL TRAITS.

DOGS ARE DESCENDED FROM WOLVES, WHICH
WERE DOMESTICATED IN PALAEOLITHIC TIMES.

LIKE HUMANS, WOLVES
NURTURE THEIR YOUNG, A
HABIT THAT MADE THEM
PRIME CANDIDATES
FOR DOMESTICATION.

13

survived by cooperative hunting of game, and wolves behave in the same way.

So the domestication of wolves came about because they shared a number of habits and needs with humans and, as cubs, pandered to the human need to tend to small, helpless creatures. As wolves and humans lived closer together, they developed a mutual understanding. Wolves became more sociable and relaxed around human beings, learning to respond to commands; while, over time, humans exploited wolf behaviour, using wolves to assist in hunting and to guard their homes.

Climate change and the emergence of settled, rather than nomadic, societies were also important factors in wolf domestication. Wolf cubs are reliant on their mother until they are four or five months old. They live in semipermanent dens and their mother must commute between the cubs and sources of food

LONG-LIMBED AND ELEGANT, SALUKI HOUNDS ORIGINATED IN THE MIDDLE EAST.

THE MASTIFF IS ONE OF THE OLDEST DOG BREEDS.

during this time. A nomadic lifestyle thus being out of the question for wolves, domestication can be pinpointed reasonably accurately to around fourteen thousand years ago, when humans ceased to be nomadic.

So how did the domesticated wolf produce the bewildering variety of dog breeds in existence today? The answer lies simply in inbreeding. Deprived of the chance to roam and thus mate with a wide genetic mix, pet wolves living in small, isolated societies could only mate with related individuals. Humans helped by favouring wolves with useful characteristics and killing or driving away those with undesirable features. Some communities may have preferred small dogs, others large ones; one hamlet may have liked long-haired animals, the one across the river, short haired ones. Gradually, over many generations, local varieties of dogs emerged, each a distinct product of the culture from which it had originated. As people began to live in permanent settlements and to benefit from the relative prosperity and security of this lifestyle, they could afford to keep dogs as companions, not simply as working animals. They quickly saw that they could keep dogs just for their looks or temperament; the business of dog-breeding had begun.

It is clear from the images of dogs in the earliest-surviving examples of art, from ancient Assyria, Babylon, and Egypt, that they had been bred to serve different purposes. Frescoes and wall-paintings dating from 4000 BC illustrate animals that are recognizable as greyhounds, Salukis, and mastiffs, proof that distinct breeds of dogs had emerged, each with a different function. Archaeological excavations at Avebury, in Wiltshire, England, have revealed the five-thousand-year-old remains of a small, long-legged, short-backed dog, a complete contrast to the great Babylonian mastiff. These remains are also evidence that as humans became more fond of dogs in life, they chose to be buried near to them in death

working dogs

Human beings began to breed a variety of types of dog suited to widely differing tasks, not all of which were utilitarian. Dogs were also bred for aesthetic purposes, or to accentuate certain attractive or novel physical features. People tried to develop existing aggressive canine traits by breeding pugnacious dogs to fight either each other or other animals, such as bears or bulls. Charles Darwin explained the principles of breeding to enhance genetic characteristics in *The Origin of Species*:

"Thus it is known that a cross with a bulldog has affected for many generations the courage and obstinacy of greyhounds; and a cross with a greyhound has given a whole family of sheep-dogs a tendency to hunt hares. These domestic instincts, when thus tested by crossing resemble natural instincts, which in a like manner become curiously blended together, and for a long period exhibit traces of the instincts of either parent…"

HUNTERS

Wolves and humans hunted similar prey, and Palaeolithic man may well have followed hunting wolves and then intercepted them as they captured their game. However, this would have been a time-consuming method of hunting, and although even today Aboriginals in Australia exploit dingoes' hunting skills, it is an occasional, opportunistic means of acquiring food. The earliest evidence of dogs assisting in human hunting comes from ancient Egypt, with reliefs and wall-paintings showing dogs virtually identical to the modern basenji, a hunting breed widely prevalent in Africa today. The ancient Egyptians, or their forebears, had obviously bred a dog specifically for hunting, and the dog's superior natural abilities to find and retrieve game became increasingly important.

Dogs have accompanied human hunters for centuries, and require little training in what, for them, is a natural inclination. Hunting for pleasure was adopted by the aristocracies of ancient China, India, Persia, and Egypt and spread throughout medieval Europe. It continues to be popular among the leisured classes today, although it has become a matter of some controversy in Britain. Dogs' highly developed sense of smell enables them to sniff out game for their masters to trap, spear, or shoot. Canine hunting skills evolved and altered as humans adopted different weapons: the introduction of guns, for example, meant that dogs were trained in setting and retrieving techniques.

ALTHOUGH PUGNACIOUS IN APPEARANCE, BULLDOGS ARE EXTREMELY GOOD-NATURED.

BORZOIS WERE BRED IN RUSSIA FOR WOLF-HUNTING.

DEERHOUNDS ORIGINATED IN SCOTLAND.

LABRADOR RETRIEVERS ARE EASY TO TRAIN.

THE DOBERMAN MAKES AN EXCELLENT GUARD DOG.

INTELLIGENT GERMAN SHEPHERDS MAKE GOOD
GUARD DOGS.

DALMATIANS ARE ENERGETIC AND AFFECTIONATE.

TRACKERS

Dogs possess a sense of smell that is far more efficient than that in humans. Rescue dogs can be trained to track a scent on the ground and others can follow a scent in the air; hunting dogs, such as retrievers and pointers, can not only track birds, but can distinguish one type from another. Bloodhounds are the archetypal "sniffer dogs" and have the ability to follow a trail tenaciously for hours. The Red Cross still uses dogs to sniff out injured people on battlefields or in disaster zones. In recent times, dogs such as German shepherds and Labrador retrievers have been trained to sniff out drugs and explosives and to track missing persons, often with great success.

GUARD DOGS

The dog's pack mentality means that if it senses the arrival of strangers – human or otherwise – it will alert the other members of the pack. When they are alarmed or excited, domestic dogs react by barking, which is a distinct difference from their vulpine counterparts, who bark only in moments of extreme alarm. It is evident from Babylonian art that mastiffs were very popular as criminal deterrents. They were reportedly given intimidating names, such as "Expeller of the Sinful" and "Hesitate Not," monikers that are not so very different from the modern habit of naming fierce-looking dogs "Tyson," after the renowned boxer.

The dog's natural ability as a runner prompted people to use dogs to run alongside their carriages during the eighteenth and nineteenth centuries – when the carriage stopped, the dogs were present to protect the travellers. Two hundred years ago, Dalmatians were bred specifically for this purpose, their black-and-white coats usefully merging with the shadows at night, making them invisible to footmen and highwaymen.

Dogs continue to prove their value as guards. Police forces in a number of countries train Dobermans, which are excellent patrol dogs, and German shepherds, which can learn to guard, attack, and "arrest" suspects, gripping a subject firmly, but without injury, until law-enforcement personnel arrive. Well-trained dogs are immensely valuable to the police, the prison service, or any authority seeking to control big crowds. They are very useful in guarding large areas, such as airfields, because they are fast runners, while their agility means that they can squeeze into inaccessible places and their powers of scenting and hearing are infinitely superior to those of their human masters.

DOGS OF WAR

Dogs have performed valiant service in times of war. Man's inhumanity to man looms large from the pages of history, so it is not surprising that this inhumanity has been inflicted on humankind's closest animal companion, too. The dog's natural inclination to protect and guard was exploited in large dogs, and the more ferocious were used as dogs of war, to harass enemies and protect armies. During the Peloponnesian War (431–404 BC), the barking of a dog named Sorter alerted Corinth to a stealth attack, and the grateful citizens later erected a monument to this vigilant animal.

The Spanish Conquistadors travelled to the New World with mastiffs with which to intimidate and hunt down the native people, dogs furthermore playing a critical part in many campaigns because they were adept at breaking up ambushes in dense forests. First employed by the Spanish as early as 1493, dogs proved horribly effective. Among the most famous was Becerrillo ("Little Calf"), who reputedly killed so many men that he earned an additional share of the booty for his master, Juan Ponce de León. Other Conquistadors, including Hernando Cortés, executed their prisoners by turning the "dogs of war" on them.

Dogs continue to be trained to perform a variety of wartime tasks, some more acceptable than others. During the Second World War, for example, the Soviet Red Army strapped anti-tank mines to its dogs' backs and trained them to seek out German tanks. Unfortunately, the dogs had not been trained in the finer points of tank recognition and, when released on to the battlefield, indiscriminately aimed for the Soviet tanks as well.

STURDY ROTTWEILERS ARE BRAVE GUARD DOGS.

AIREDALES ARE THE LARGEST TERRIERS.

GIANT SCHNAUZERS ORIGINATED AS HERDING DOGS.

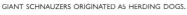

HERDERS

Dogs were probably used as guardians of cattle and sheep very early on in their relationship with people. In Sumerian scrolls dating from 5000 BC, the dog-headed goddess Bau was described as a protector of flocks; it is likely that the name of the goddess was derived from the sound of a dog's bark. The earliest sheepdogs were probably valued more for their ferocity in scaring away predators and thieves than for their capacity to herd livestock. The Roman writer Marcus Tarentius Varo noted in 10 BC in *De Re Rustica* that, "There are two kinds [of dog], one for hunting connected with the wild beasts of the woods, the other trained for purposes of defense, and used by shepherds."

Herding breeds vary across the world according to geographical location: because they have to deal with different animals in every type of terrain, herding dogs are the product of local breeding in order to meet the needs of a particular area. Ancient breeds of flock-guarding sheepdogs are still employed in parts of Europe and Asia, such as the savage Tibetan mastiff, the komondor and Kuvasz from Hungary, and the Pyrenean mountain

POPULAR DOGS, BRIARDS WERE FRENCH SHEEPDOGS.

TOUGH AND HARDY, THE KELPIE IS AN AUSTRALIAN SHEEPDOG.

THE TIBETAN MASTIFF IS A FIERCE DEFENDER.

TOY POODLES ARE INTELLIGENT AND LONG-LIVED.

SIBERIAN HUSKIES ARE TOUGH WORKING DOGS.

GREYHOUNDS ARE THE FASTEST DOG BREED.

dog, none of whom appear as reliable and steady as the Old English sheepdog, for example.

Smaller than most of the European herding breeds, collies are probably the most commonly used sheepdogs in Britain, particularly the highly intelligent Border collie, which has succeeded its cousin, the Rough collie (immortalized on film as Lassie during the 1950s). Formal sheepdog training begins when a dog is six months old, and the dog is encouraged to get used to being around sheep before actually herding them. The Old English sheepdog was more often used to drive sheep and cattle to market than to herd them. Australia has produced the kelpie, an energetic working dog tough enough to cope with the demands of rough terrain and extremes of temperature.

CENTURIES OF WORK

Many dogs demonstrate a desire to please their human masters, and over the years this desire has been exploited by training dogs to do an amazing range of tasks. "Comforters" were small lapdogs that were once used to attract the fleas and lice that would otherwise have infested their owners, while "turnspits" were dogs trained to turn the great roasting spit over an open fire. However, as society changes, so, too, do the uses of dogs, and today guide dogs, sniffer dogs, and working dogs are indispensable.

Motorized transport has diminished the use of dogs as beasts of burden and transport, but in some areas of the world dogs are still used for this purpose by people, such as the North American Inuit, who traditionally employ sled dogs. Characterized by a sharply pointed muzzle, broad skull, and pointed ears, sled dogs like Siberian huskies have powerful bodies and thick, rough coats. In the harsh environment of the Arctic Circle, teams of huskies often prove more reliable than mechanical transport, which may break down in the extreme cold.

Laws have been passed either to control dogs or to prohibit certain classes of society from owning them. During the eleventh century, for example, King Canute banned greyhounds from the game-packed English royal forests to prevent poaching. The Tudors and Stuarts used heavy fines to control dog ownership, and during the Great Plague of 1665 over forty thousand dogs were slaughtered to halt the spread of the disease (which was spread by fleas living on rats, and presumably also on dogs, although, ironically, the dogs could have assisted in killing the rats). More recently, in 1991 the British government passed the Dangerous Dogs Act, making it a criminal offence for a dog to be out of control in a public place.

SOCIAL WORK

One of the most famous roles of the working dog is as a guide dog for blind people. It is likely that dogs have accompanied blind people for centuries—

Charles Dickens remarks on one such case during the mid-nineteenth century – but properly trained dogs were first used after the First World War, when German soldiers, blinded in the hostilities in France, were given specially trained dogs as companions to help them return to civilian life. Golden and black Labrador retrievers are today most commonly used as guide dogs, along with German shepherds. In Britain, such dogs are bred by the Guide Dogs for the Blind charity from bitches specially chosen for their intelligence and equable temperament. The average working life of a guide dog is eight or nine years, and its training is rigorous, beginning when the dog is six weeks old. Puppies begin their training with a sighted "puppy-walker," who accustoms the dog to buses, trains, urban scenes, and crowds – everyday situations encountered by a blind person. When the dog is a year old, it begins the next phase of its training at a guide-dog centre, where it learns how to deal with crossing roads and coping with traffic and to judge height and width so that its owner does not bump into obstacles.

Dogs have also been trained to support deaf people, for instance, to alert their owners to an important sound, such as a boiling kettle or a telephone, by touching them and leading them to the source of the noise. Research has proved that elderly, lonely, or distressed people benefit from the companionship of a dog, and charities like the British Pets as Therapy (PAT) provide friendly, reliable dogs to visit hospices or residential homes to cheer people of all ages.

The Far East, however, is an exception. Here dogs are more often seen on menus than with their owners. Dogs were once farmed as a food source in parts of China, Polynesia, and Central America, a custom that was probably a means of coping with chronic shortages of any other animal protein. (It may be significant that cannibalism was also prevalent in the same areas, possibly for the same reason.) Domestic dogs treat humans as members of their own species, and people in return endow their dogs with human characteristics, real or imagined, which is probably why dog-eating is regarded with extreme distaste in many cultures.

RACING AND COMPETITION DOGS

It is in the nature of dogs to run around, and dog-racing began in Roman times as hare-coursing, a sport that is still practised today using greyhounds, whippets, and lurchers. Greyhound-racing using a fake hare first occurred in Britain in 1876, but the sport died out because the runners simply finished too closely together. After the First World War, however, an Oklahoma farmer discovered a patent for a mechanical hare and built a circular track, after which greyhound-racing quickly became popular and was reintroduced to Britain in 1924.

Competitive sled-racing began in Alaska during the 1880s, using teams of Siberian huskies and Eskimo

GOLDEN RETRIEVERS ARE EQUABLE DOGS,
IDEAL FOR FAMILIES.

HUSKY RACING IS A POPULAR SPORT IN NORTHERN CLIMES.

WHIPPETS WERE BRED AS RACING DOGS.

ITALIAN GREYHOUNDS LOVE TO CHASE.

LARGE ELEGANT DOGS, GREYHOUNDS LIKE TO INHABIT A SPECIAL CORNER OF THEIR HOME.

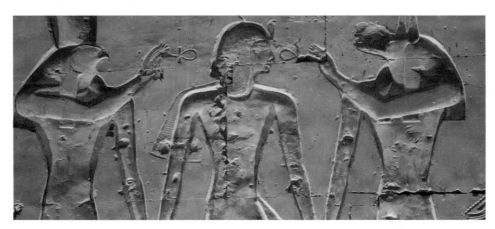

DOGS WERE IMPORTANT TO THE ANCIENT EGYPTIANS WHO BELIEVED THEY POSSESSED SUPERNATURAL ABILITIES !

malamutes. It remains an exceptionally popular sport in North America and Northern Europe, to the extent that racing continues after the snow has melted with sleds mounted on rollerblades.

As obedience training has grown in importance and popularity, the establishment of show and obedience trials has been enthusiastically received all over the world. Dogs can demonstrate their achievement of a certain level of training in these and, if they are really good, can win extra awards and titles. The initial level emphasizes basic training, with a dog showing that it can walk at heel and obey simple spoken commands. At the highest level, dogs demonstrate their skills in tracking and scenting tests.

dogs in myth and legend

The importance of dogs to humans is underlined by the fact that dogs feature in the mythology and legends of just about every culture, from Celtic through Native American to ancient Greek. Certain characteristics stand out in canine mythology: dogs are invariably loyal, faithful, and steadfast helpers of people; it is only if they appear in an unusual form (such as the three-headed Cerberus) that they pose a serious threat.

The ancient Egyptians believed that dogs possessed supernatural qualities and pampered them by giving them servants and the finest food. Only royalty could own pedigree dogs, and when the pharaoh died, his dog was often buried with him to provide him with protection in the afterlife. Just as the ancient Egyptians believed that dogs followed their owners into the afterlife, many cultures regarded dogs as mediators between the realms of the living and the dead: the Egyptian underworld god Anubis was depicted with a jackal's head, for example, while Cerberus, the three-headed dog, was said to guard Hades, the underworld of ancient Greek mythology. In the Zoroastrian religion, corpses are quickly removed to sacred ground, where a priest prays and a dog and a sacred fire keep evil forces at bay.

The Celts believed that dogs had curative powers, as did the Greeks, who linked them to Aesclepius, the god of healing. Dogs were kept at Epidaurus, the shrine of Aesclepius, and the god was sometimes shown accompanied by a dog who could reputedly cure illness by licking the afflicted person.

Dogs recur throughout classical literature. In The Odyssey, Homer says that Ulysses' faithful dog, Argus, recognized his master on his return from Troy when no one else could—and then died of joy. Horace mentions that the sight of a black dog with its pups was considered unlucky.

Many Roman legends recount tales of dogs' fidelity, but the Romans also sacrificed dogs at the annual festival of Robigalia, which was intended to protect cornfields from too much heat or blight during the summer. The Romans clearly linked dogs with great

dogs in art
and literature

heat, calling the six or eight hottest days of summer *caniculares dies*, "dog days," and believing that Sirius, the "Dog Star," rose with the sun and added to its

heat, the "dog days" thus combining the heat of the sun with the apparent warmth of the exceptionally bright Dog Star. In Greco-Roman mythology, the dog Sirius was sacred to the messenger god Hermes (Mercury) and Artemis (Diana), the goddess of the hunt; he also accompanied Hekate (Hecate), signifying war, and Orion the hunter.

The dog was important in Chinese folklore and was regarded in much the same way as black cats in European superstition. In China, the "Fu Dog," a symbol of good luck and happiness, is traditionally placed at the front door to ward off evil spirits.

The three great monotheistic religions are, at best, indifferent to dogs. In Judeo-Christian tradition, dogs rarely receive a good word, while Islam regards them as unclean creatures and requires its adherents to cleanse themselves after coming into contact with them. Like many Islamic laws, however, this one is based on common sense: rabies has long been prevalent throughout the Near and Middle East, so it is prudent to ensure that one does not become contaminated with it through an infected dog's saliva.

Writers as illustrious as Homer and Horace, Sir Thomas More, Alexander Pope, Mark Twain, and James Thurber have all proffered advice about dog care, expressed their affection for their pets, and noted their habits and foibles.

One of the best-loved dogs appears in J.M. Barrie's *Peter Pan*. The Darling children's nurse is Nana, a Newfoundland, hired because the family was too poor to afford a human nanny, but who "proved to be quite a treasure of a nurse ... It was a lesson in propriety to see her escorting the children to school, walking sedately by their side when they were well behaved, and butting them back into line if they strayed."

Dog-owners have been keen to immortalize their pets virtually since the animal was first domesticated, and dogs can be seen in Palaeolithic paintings and are also represented in ancient Egyptian art, their stylized images appearing in classical Greek sculpture, too. In medieval art, a dog symbolizes fidelity, and in many medieval funerary monuments a dog is placed at the feet of a woman's effigy to represent affection and fidelity. Although male funerary effigies often had a lion at their feet to represent the manly virtues of courage and valour, some Crusaders are shown with their feet resting on dogs, symbolizing the fact that they followed the standard of Christ as faithfully as a dog follows his master. Dogs appeared in miniature in medieval

THE NEWFOUNDLAND HAS A WELL-DESERVED
REPUTATION AS A RELIABLE AND FRIENDLY BREED.

SHEEPDOGS ARE USED TO SELL A BRAND OF PAINT.

illuminated manuscripts and tapestries, too, most famously the Bayeaux Tapestry, in which King Harold of England is shown out hawking with five dogs.

By the time of the Renaissance, dogs were featuring in many different styles of picture. They added a pleasing sense of normality both to formal portraits, such as Jan van Eyck's *Arnolfini Wedding* (1434), and to depictions of great religious scenes. A greyhound can be seen hunting in the background of Benozzo Gozzoli's *The Journey of the Magi to Bethlehem* (c. 1459–63), for example, seemingly unaware of the great men passing a few feet away as it rushes onward. In the same picture,

the Magi's military escort is accompanied by a black-and tan hound, who has the alert air of a guard dog.

Dogs appeared in both hunting and formal portraits of the great men and women of the sixteenth and seventeenth centuries. The nobility of Europe wished to be recorded for posterity surrounded by items of value, or possessions that

DALMATIANS—ONE IS SUFFICIENT FOR MOST HOMES.

A BLOODHOUND IMMORTALIZED HUSH PUPPY SHOES.

A POODLE WITH A SMART CONTINENTAL CUT.

lent them status, and small lapdogs often appear in the court portraits of Velásquez and Van Dyck, as do long-limbed hunting dogs beside their beautifully clad masters. By the eighteenth century, fashions had changed, and dogs were illustrated in their own right. The works of notable artists such George Stubbs, famed for his animal portraits, are testimony to the esteem in which pet dogs were held by their wealthy owners.

By the nineteenth and early twentieth centuries, dogs were being depicted on magazine covers and postcards, as china figurines and in cartoons. They were also popular choices for advertisements: Hush Puppy shoes adopted a bloodhound, Dulux paint employs an Old English sheepdog, while Andrex toilet paper uses an impossibly cute Labrador puppy, but the longest-lived must surely be Nipper, a terrier shown faithfully listening to a gramophone in the logo for HMV records (HMV stands for "His Master's Voice").

celluloid canines

As Hollywood turned a giant mirror on the world and reflected life back at us as entertainment, dogs inevitably had a large role to play. The first great canine star of the silver screen was Rin Tin Tin, a German shepherd dog who starred in twenty-two silent movies. Rescued by an American airman in France in 1918, Rin Tin Tin was, by all accounts, an exceptional dog. He excelled at stunts, would stand still for thirty minutes so that the studio lighting could be adjusted and had an excellent relationship with his owner, Lee Duncan, who said, "We simply understand each other, and until you understand your dog you can never hope to teach him anything." In 1947, fifteen years after his death, Rin Tin Tin was "revived" for a television series that was just as popular as the original movies.

Lassie, a Rough collie with a luxurious coat and super-canine intelligence, was the other great canine cinematic success story. Pal, the dog who played Lassie, lived an enviably pampered life in his own apartment and had stunt-doubles to stand in for him during the dangerous scenes.

Dogs have peppered every genre of movie, from Dorothy's feisty terrier, Toto, in The Wizard of Oz (1939) to the narcotics cop's German shepherd in K9 (1988). Because they embody faithfulness, companionship, and utter reliability, dogs tend to be typecast: Dobermans are invariably portrayed as savage, extravagantly clipped poodles as slightly ridiculous, while Labradors are brave and beloved by children. Anthropomorphism plays its part, too. Films like The Incredible Journey (1963), also known as "two dogs and a cat" to many toddlers) endow the dogs with very different characters: the old Labrador retriever is eminently sensible and trusts his human masters; the young bull terrier is impulsive, cocky and excitable. The third animal star, the cat, is simply too cool for words. This characterization of dogs and cats is taken to extremes in Cats and Dogs (2001), a movie whose central feature is the enjoyable conceit that the world is ruled by, yes, cats and dogs, who con humans into thinking that they are pliable companions. How ridiculous is that?

TWO

the canine world

No species on Earth is more diverse than the dog. Originally intended to be reasonably fast hunting animals, many breeds now struggle to work up much of a pace and prefer a gentle walk around the block rather than a vigorous run. Human intervention rather than natural selection has worked to produce the huge range of shapes and sizes that exist today. Indeed, many breeds would die out extremely quickly if left to themselves; the respiratory problems and whelping difficulties among bulldogs provide just one example. Human tinkering, however, is unable to replace the basic genetic characteristics that form the building blocks of canine physiology and psychology, and all dogs, regardless of their breed, share a number of fundamental characteristics.

They have efficient cardiovascular systems designed for running, with deep rib cages to protect their vital organs. They have highly developed sensory organs to underline their role as natural hunters and defenders of territory. With efficient, sensitive hearing, and a highly refined sense of smell, even the smallest dog will bark as a warning when strangers approach. All dogs, like their vulpine ancestors, are pack animals, genetically programmed to respect the hierarchy of their pack or family. They feel secure knowing their place in the pack, which explains why dogs readily accept the dominance of their human owners.

THE POWERFULLY BUILT ELKHOUND (ABOVE LEFT) HAS A DENSE, WEATHER-PROOF COAT, QUITE UNLIKE THE LOOSE FOLDS OF SKIN AND EXTREMELY SHORT, STRAIGHT COAT OF THE SHAR PEI (ABOVE RIGHT).

canine physiology

Despite their great range of shapes and sizes, all dogs share the same genetic and physical specification. Dogs are quadruped mammals, with a musculature, limb structure, and cardiovascular system designed for running. They have thirty-nine pairs of chromosomes (compared to humans' twenty-three pairs), a skeleton consisting of three-hundred-and-nineteen bones, and forty-two adult teeth, which are perfectly designed for shredding flesh and tearing food. The structure of their limbs and muscles is intended to enable them (or their ancestral wild dogs) to run on their toes for long periods without tiring. Their heart and lungs are large in order to cope with the need to supply blood and oxygen to an energetic body. In short, nature intended dogs to be hunters.

Dog sizes vary tremendously: the Irish wolfhound, for example, measures about 32 in (1 m) at the withers, whereas the Chihuahua stands at 5 in (12 cm). The color and thickness of coats vary from the gloriously coiffed Afghan hound to the less than hirsute Mexican hairless dog. The shape of a dog is determined primarily by its head, body, and legs, and the size of these differs considerably from breed to breed.

THE CHINESE CRESTED IS ENTIRELY HAIRLESS, APART FROM THE EXTRAVAGANT TUFT OF HAIR ON THE HEAD.

CHIHUAHUAS ARE THE WORLD'S SMALLEST DOGS.

IRISH WOLFHOUNDS ARE THE TALLEST DOGS.

THE AFGHAN HOUND HAS A DISTINCTIVE SHAGGY COAT.

PEKINGESE HAVE PROFUSE, THICK COATS.

Humans have altered various canine characteristics through selective breeding. The German shepherd dog, the breed closest to the dog's vulpine ancestor, possesses all of the characteristics of a well-balanced dog: a long-haired coat, well-muscled limbs to power prolonged bursts of running, and a long muzzle enclosing a range of teeth for gripping and shredding. Other breeds are less fortunate, however. Although selective breeding can accentuate useful characteristics, such as the ability to run faster, it can also produce breeds with shorter life expectancies and hereditary disorders. Bulldogs, for example, have bandy legs and squashed faces and may experience breathing difficulties; Irish setters are prone to an incurable, inherited, eye disease; while King Charles spaniels are 50 percent more likely than other breeds to be suffering from heart defects by the age of five.

THE SKIN AND COAT

With a few exceptions, dogs are covered in hair, which may be straight or wavy. The hair follicles are attached to tiny muscles that cause the hairs to bristle at times of stress. In addition, sensitive whiskers are sited near the nose.

Coats vary a great deal in dogs – more so than in any other species of domestic animal – and the type is a good indication of the geographical origin of a breed. Dogs have two textures of hair, the top coat or guard hair and the undercoat or down, and the relative thickness and distribution of these hair textures governs the style of coat. The density of both types of hair varies tremendously between breeds, too. Long, warm coats are common in breeds originating

from Northern Asia, such as the Pekingese, whose appearance is in complete contrast to the sleek, short-haired Rhodesian ridgeback, an African dog. Dogs from warm climates often possess short coats, with a high density of almost waterproof hair that provides good insulation. Wire-haired breeds have coats with thick guard hairs, which provide an excellent all-weather barrier, as well as protection against bites from other animals.

Many breeds shed their hairs seasonally, although this cycle depends to some extent on temperature, length of daylight hours, hormonal factors, nutrition, and genetic predisposition. In fall, as the days become shorter, dogs' coats usually become thicker and the hairs longer; hairs are then shed in the spring, when the dense winter undercoat becomes redundant. Growth is slowest during the summer months.

Dogs' paws are covered by an extra-tough epidermis, with a tough, protective epidermal layer on the footpads. Sweat-producing glands help maintain the footpads' suppleness, although the footpads are not sensitive to heat or cold.

THE SKELETON

Canine skeletons are robust structures that provide an excellent framework for the body. A strong skull incorporates protective pockets for the eyes and ears, and the neck vertebrae have extensions attached to powerful muscles. The shoulder blades are attached to the rest of the skeleton only by muscle, which allows enormous flexibility for running. Long ribs form a protective cage around the vital organs and the shoulders and hips act as pivots, allowing the limbs to move gracefully and accurately. The weight distribution between the front and hind legs is relatively equal.

The bones are anchored together by ligaments, while tendons attach muscles to the skeleton. Canine tendons are well developed and tendon injuries are rare, although excessive weight can cause some ligaments to tear. The weakest link is often a hind knee, which may be the source of trouble in a limping, overweight, middle-aged dog.

There are three basic head shapes: a narrow skull with a long face (the dolichocephalic skull of the Saluki, for example); a wide skull with a long face (like the mesocephalic head of the pointer); and a wide head and short muzzle (such as the boxer's brachycephalic skull, which is taken to its extreme in the short-nosed pug, which has virtually no muzzle at all).

The earliest dogs were probably about the same size as dingoes, and finished growing at the age of ten months. Mastiffs, which were first bred about five-and-a-half thousand years ago, did not mature until the age of eighteen months.

GUNDOGS LIKE THE GERMAN LONG-HAIRED POINTER GENER-ALLY HAVE WIDE HEADS AND LONG MUZZLES.

BOXERS HAVE POWERFUL, WIDE HEADS.

SALUKI HOUNDS HAVE NARROW SKULLS.

MASTIFFS HAVE BROAD SKULLS AND WIDE-SET EYES.

PUGS ARE PRIZED FOR THEIR SHORT NOSES.

Today, larger breeds reach maturity later than smaller ones.

Most dogs are well equipped to run over long distances. The configuration of their shoulder and pelvic bones, and the articulation of their leg bones and spine, allow most breeds to move fast with ease. Some breeds have been bred to emphasize a specific gait: the German shepherd, for example, is known for its "flying trot," which makes it look as though it is soaring through the air, although one foot always remains in contact with the ground. Greyhounds, which have been bred for speed, are most comfortable when galloping. Their spines are exceptionally flexible, allowing them to extend all four legs at once, with all four paws off the ground.

Despite their size, Afghan hounds, which were bred to chase game over rocky terrain, are able to turn in extremely small spaces because of the flexibility of their hip joints and lower back. Short-legged dachshunds were bred to hunt badgers underground, and their sausage-like shape enables them to dive down narrow tunnels in search of prey.

THE MUSCULAR SYSTEM

Healthy dogs display coordinated movement and a smooth, flexible gait controlled by the three muscle groups: smooth muscle, which controls movement of the viscera; cardiac muscle, which governs the heart tissue; and skeletal muscle, which the dog can control and which enables it to move.

GERMAN POINTERS HAVE STRONG JAWS AND NECKS.

The most powerful skeletal muscles are sited in the jaw, giving a dog the strength to bite or hold firmly, and in the thighs, providing instant propulsive energy for running. The neck muscles allow the head to turn more than 220 degrees, and both the ears and the tail are well muscled to enable social signaling. Muscle shrinkage occurs either through underuse or, more rarely, if the nerve supply is damaged. Regular daily exercise is therefore vital to ensure fluid muscular movement, especially for young dogs, who require two periods of exercise per day. Jumping is excellent exercise for lean dogs, but note that heavier, older animals could damage their spinal cord if they land awkwardly.

THE CARDIOVASCULAR SYSTEM

Dogs are natural runners, and their highly efficient cardiovascular system is both adept at producing vast amounts of oxygen during exercise and at dealing with the resulting waste products.

Different parts of the body require varying amounts of nourishment at different times, and the heart pumps oxygen-bearing blood around the body in response to its needs. The dog's brain receives anything from 10 to 20 percent of the blood pumped by the heart, and this figure remains constant whatever the dog is doing. During exercise, up to 90 percent of the blood pumped by the heart can be diverted to the muscles to provide the animal with extra stamina.

Blood cells collect waste products as they circulate around the body and carry them to the liver for detoxification. They are then carried to the lungs, where carbon dioxide is expelled and replaced by nourishing oxygen. Fresh red blood cells travel

through the arteries to release this oxygen into the tissue cells.

THE DIGESTION

The canine mouth is typical of a carnivorous scavenger. Six pairs of incisor teeth are positioned at the front of the mouth for nibbling, cutting, and grooming, flanked by two pairs of canines, which are used for biting and tearing at food (or prey). The canines have extremely long roots and are very sturdy teeth. The remaining teeth are premolars, used

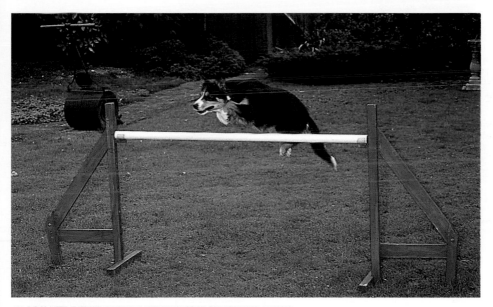

ALL DOGS NEED EXERCISE. JUMPING IS ESPECIALLY GOOD FOR YOUNGER ANIMALS.

for shredding and cutting, and molars, for chewing and grinding.

The canine tongue is comparatively thin and is mainly used for the processing of food, for cleaning the coat, and for perspiring. (Hot dogs cool down by letting their tongues hang out and panting. Panting causes moisture to evaporate from the tongue, which cools the skin. Dogs also sweat through the pads on their paws.)

Dogs' gastrointestinal systems are designed to deal with large amounts of food received infrequently and irregularly – although most domestic animals today enjoy regular meals. Dogs rarely chew their food, instead gulping or swallowing it so that it passes directly through the aesophagus and into the stomach, where it is broken down by digestive enzymes. The food then leaves the stomach through the pyloric sphincter and moves into the small intestine. Most of the digestion and absorption of food occurs in the small intestine, aided by the pancreas and the liver. The pancreas regulates the digestive process by secreting enzymes, as well as insulin and glucagons to regulate glucose levels. As in humans, the liver is the largest internal organ in the dog's body. It has six lobes (compared to humans' two) and produces bile to help the absorption of fat, as well as metabolizing proteins and carbohydrates. It excretes toxins from the blood and manufactures blood-clotting agents. These are all vitally important functions, and liver disease can be a major problem in dogs.

From the small intestine, any remaining food shifts to the large intestine, which contains large numbers of bacteria. These guard against infection, break down waste material, and process vitamins. Once digestion is complete, waste matter is defaecated.

THE URINARY AND REPRODUCTIVE SYSTEMS

Further waste matter is dealt with by the kidneys, which hang from the roof of the abdomen and are protected by the dog's bottom ribs. The kidneys filter toxic substances from the blood, clear waste then passing into the renal pelvis through two ureters to the bladder. The urethra discharges urine from the penis or through the vulva.

Dogs reach sexual maturity between six and twelve months of age, although emotional maturity is not achieved until about eighteen months. A female dog who has puppies very young may not have the emotional resources to cope with being a good mother, so it is important to ensure that she does not mate during her first oestrus cycle.

Male dogs are always sexually active, constantly on the lookout for a willing mate, to whom they are attracted by scent. Females ovulate only twice a year. During the pro-oestrus cycle, lasting about twelve days, a female dog's vulva swells and produces a discharge. This is followed by five days of oestrus, when eggs are released into the Fallopian tubes, and it is at this point that she chooses a mate. The ovaries remain active for life. (See also the section on breeding, pages 171 to 174.)

UNABLE TO SWEAT EXCEPT THROUGH THEIR PAW PADS, DOGS PANT
TO HELP THEM COOL DOWN.

BOXERS' EYES ARE FRONT-SET.

GREYHOUNDS HAVE GOOD PERIPHERAL VISION.

DOGS HAVE A HIGHLY DEVELOPED SENSE OF SMELL.

DOGS USE BODY LANGUAGE TO COMMUNICATE.

THE SENSES

A dog's five senses are attuned very differently to those of humans. The canine sense of smell is sensitive, sophisticated, and the dog's most acute sense. It is for this reason that dogs are employed to track missing persons or to sniff out contraband drugs or explosives. Some breeds have a more highly developed olfactory sense than others: that of German shepherds and bloodhounds, for example, is far more efficient than that of short-nosed breeds, such as pugs.

It is estimated that dogs' sense of smell is at least a hundred times better than humans' (and may be as high as 100 million times more efficient). The average dog possesses over 200 million scent receptors (humans have 5 million), and the area of the brain devoted to smell is correspondingly larger.

Dogs famously have damp noses, and the moisture helps to capture scent and transmit it to the nasal membranes sited on the thin turbinate bones within the nose. Convoluted folds within these bones trap the scent and send messages to the olfactory-bulb region of the brain. The vomeronasal organ, situated in the roof of a dog's mouth, is devoted entirely to sex-scenting, enabling a dog to identify a suitable mate.

Body odours are produced by a number of secretions and glands in the dog's body, from saliva, ear secretions, vaginal, and preputial discharges and from glands around the anus and on top of the tail. All provide information about the sexual status of the animal and are used to scent-mark territory. The anal-sac glands deposit a drop of pheromone-enriched liquid on top of faeces, which is as distinct to each individual as fingerprints in humans.

By contrast, the canine sense of taste is quite poor. Humans have six times as many taste buds as dogs, and the tongues of dogs appear almost rough because the surface is covered with lumpy papillae, which house the taste receptors. If left to their own devices and forced to scavenge for food, dogs will eat almost anything. They are initially attracted to food by smell, after which taste and texture receptors take over. Dogs can taste sour or acid foods over the whole tongue, sweet tastes at the sides, salt along the sides and at the base, but water only at the tip.

Hearing in dogs is very acute. They are able to hear sounds well beyond the range of the human ear, often from a great distance. Many aboriginal breeds possessed large, erect ears, and canine ears are generally mobile, enabling them to detect sounds four times farther away than humans can hear. Dogs are also capable of shutting off their inner ear in order to filter out distracting noises.

More than any other body part, the shape of dogs' ears has been modified by selective breeding. The natural shape is erect and mobile, like wolves' ears, and some breeds retain this, giving them an air of alertness. At the other extreme, however, are the pendulous ears of ground-scenting dogs like the bloodhound. Some breeds, such as the greyhound, have "rose" ears, which can be raised or folded back when running.

Dogs are sensitive to touch. Whiskers (known as vibrissae) around the muzzle, which can be moved voluntarily, are equipped with many nerve fibres and can sense air flow. Dogs use touch and smell to communicate with one another, and touch plays an important part in bonding with a dog. Dogs huddle together for warmth and use licking and pawing as a means of establishing dominance.

Canine vision is less acute than dogs' sense of smell. They have proportionately larger corneas than humans, which means that their night vision is highly efficient, but the mixture of rods and cones in the central area of their retinas allows only poor colour definition and generally less acute eyesight. The position of dogs' eyes varies among breeds. Many hunting dogs, such as whippets and greyhounds, have eyes set at the sides of their heads, giving them excellent peripheral vision that is ideal for hunting and chasing. The eyes of other breeds, such as bloodhounds and boxers, for example, are positioned more frontally, giving them good binocular vision.

The dog possesses a "third" eyelid, a membrane layer at the inner angle of the eyelid that generally protects the eye from irritants. It cannot be moved voluntarily, but shifts across the eye when the eye is pulled deeper into the socket by muscle action.

Many animals are credited with a sixth sense that enables them to know when natural disasters are about to occur or, more prosaically, when a member of the family is approaching. Dogs are intelligent creatures, and many dog-owners believe that their pets can judge their moods or that they try to tell them when something is wrong. Scientific studies have revealed that dogs possess an electromagnetic sense that makes them aware of earth tremors and vibrations and that may enable them to travel great distances to find their way home.

BLOODHOUNDS HAVE THE BEST SENSE OF SMELL.

PUGS HAVE SHORT, WRINKLED NOSES.

ALL DOGS BEGIN LIFE IN A CANINE PACK.

canine behaviour

Canine behaviour results from a combination of nature and nurture. Dogs are sociable creatures, who prefer the company of other dogs and people to living alone, while canine logic is very simple, being governed by the needs of survival and comfort. Because survival means food, tasty snacks become an important bargaining counter when training a dog. Certain behaviour, such as jumping up to lick a person's face, is governed by the basic instinct to beg for food. (Licking a mother wolf's face stimulates the regurgitation of food for the cub.)

The genetic make-up of dogs provides them with a number of basic survival instincts based on the behaviour of the pack animal. These basic instincts are modified during the dog's life, most critically during the early weeks of life. Born with a number of genetically preprogrammed characteristics, from the age of about three weeks puppies will socialize with their littermates, learning to interact with them and with people. Puppies learn by watching their mothers and, until they are twelve weeks old, absorb everything that they see, hear, taste, smell, and feel. The more it learns during these vital early weeks, the more adaptable the puppy will be as an adult dog.

Pack animals exist in a close-knit hierarchy dominated by a leader – usually a male – who controls pack activity. Fortunately, most dogs are happy to follow a dominant male, secure in the knowledge that someone else is in charge. Domestic dogs regard their owners as pack leaders and will follow them and defend their territory. Dog-owners must establish themselves as the dominant partner within the home by training their dog to follow human, rather than canine, behavioural cues. Exposure to humans when a puppy is under six weeks old will help to ensure that it will be accustomed to people and be able to learn from them.

Pack animals are sophisticated creatures who have learned a number of rules about coexisting successfully. Wolves hunt together, share food, and huddle together for warmth, increasing the chances of their own, and the pack's, survival. Puppies begin their lives in a natural pack until they leave their mother and become part of a human pack. At first, the mother is pack leader because she controls the food source and provides warmth and security. By the age of three weeks, puppies are strong enough to play, to experiment with making physical contact with each other, and to learn to test their bodies. Puppies initially learn about pack hierarchy through play. Once a puppy is removed from the mother to the care of a human, the dog-owner – the controller of food, warmth and security – becomes pack leader.

PUPPIES SHOULD BECOME ACCUSTOMED TO BEING HANDLED BY HUMANS WHEN THEY ARE VERY YOUNG.

By the time a dog has matured emotionally, at about eighteen months of age, it has usually established its status within the pack (generally a human family). A dominant dog may challenge its allocated position by refusing to obey commands or picking on the weakest member of the pack to assert itself (because this may be a child in a family household, early training to establish control over a dog is crucially important).

Dogs are extremely territorial, and within a pack each member is responsible for defending the pack's territory. Dogs respond quickly when they sense something new or strange approaching their territory, and will alert the rest of the pack (or household) by barking. Dogs may become aggressive when defending their territory, but for many owners this is desirable, security being one of the main reasons for dog-ownership.

Canine aggression takes several forms, each with different causes. Maternal aggression is the natural response of a mother trying to protect her pups.

MOTHERS TEACH THEIR YOUNG HOW TO BEHAVE AND OFTEN NIP THEM TO CONTROL BEHAVIOUR.

THIS DOG DEFENDS WHAT IS CONSIDERS TO BE ITS TERRITORY BY CHASING A CAR AWAY.

Predatory aggression is seen when a dog is catching prey, such as a rabbit or bird, or even when chasing a cat or car.

Dogs that have been trained to catch people demonstrate trained aggression, which is usually only sparked by a verbal command. Territorial aggression is a natural canine characteristic, although problems may arise if a dog actually attacks someone. Dogs usually try to intimidate opponents with a display of aggressive behaviour, but will try to avoid full-blown conflict (hence the phrase "his bark is worse than his bite").

Dogs will defend their territory against other dogs, as well as humans, and this behaviour is more common among dogs whose owners are absent, when the dog becomes extra-protective of its territory. Frightened dogs often become aggressive, while dogs being harassed by small children may bite because they misunderstand their behaviour. Males around the age of two years will often fight to establish dominance, and other dogs will defend their toys or food bowls. Persistent aggression in adult males can be solved by castration.

WHEN TWO DOGS MEET, ONE OF THEM WILL USUALLY TRY TO ESTABLISH A DOMINANT POSITION.

All dogs love playing, but less dominant dogs play more willingly and more frequently. Play is vital for dogs because it provides stimulation, exercise, encourages dexterity, and reinforces the bonds of affection between owner and pet. Play should also emphasize status: dogs must be submissive to their owners, so humans should dominate play activity.

Dogs demonstrate attachment to their human owners by bringing them "gifts" of toys or sticks or by rolling over, asking to be tickled. People interpret these types of behaviour as affection, and although they are certainly signs that a dog is feeling relaxed and happy, animal behaviourists disagree about the emotional depth of dogs' feelings.

DOGS ARE NATURALLY ALERT, FRIENDLY, AND CURIOUS ANIMALS.

UNDERSTANDING CANINE BODY LANGUAGE

MAKING EYE CONTACT IS IMPORTANT TO DOGS.

Dogs have evolved a complex range of nonverbal communication based upon body language and communication by scent. Their interaction is based upon the simple logic of pack animals and is intended to ascertain rank and establish dominance or submissiveness within the pack. The meaning of some actions is clear to humans, but others are more complicated and are still not fully understood by animal behaviourists. Dogs use their ears, faces, mouths, tails, and bodies, either independently or in combination, to convey messages to each other and to humans. Dogs are extremely expressive social creatures and there is usually enough common ground between dogs and their owners for mutual understanding. People often interpret canine communication in human terms.

Dogs' facial expressions are reasonably clear, and eye contact is an important factor. Although dogs have fewer facial muscles than humans, the mouth is a good indicator of mood: bared teeth are a sign of aggression, while the "submissive grin" is the sign of a subservient dog. Dominant dogs will stare at other individuals to establish rank, while submissive dogs will look away. Aggressive dogs exhibit erect ears, bared teeth, and a hard stare, while submissive animals have flattened ears

THIS HAPPY DOG'S EXPRESSION IS EASY TO READ!

ROLLING OVER IS A PLEA FOR TICKLING AND PLAY.

and a closed mouth. Erect ears are a sign of confidence and alertness in both friendly and aggressive dogs, and ears flattened against the head usually indicate fear or submission. Another obvious indicator is tail carriage: a tail held down, between the legs, is the sign of a fearful and submissive dog, but when held high, it indicates confidence and excitement.

A dog's posture also provides clues as to its mood, and subtle gestures are used for communication, although canine expression is limited by dogs' bodies. Dogs are restricted by their need to stand on all four legs most of the time, and they have forelegs rather than arms, so cannot demonstrate fine gestures. They can alter their centre of gravity to lean forward or backward by lowering their back legs; they can stand up, lie down, crouch, or roll over; they can make themselves look larger or smaller by raising or lowering the hairs on the back of their neck; or they can vary their posture by turning sideways or facing another animal. These postures are used in conjunction with facial expressions, scenting, and tail carriage.

An aggressive or frightened dog will raise its hackles in an attempt to appear bigger and, when on the verge of attack, will take up a forward stance, with its ears raised. Frightened dogs assume a backward stance, leaning back, tail down, lips bared, and ears back, although, if cornered, the dog may become more aggressive. A submissive dog almost crouches, with its eyes averted, ears back, and tail down and, if really overwhelmed, it will lie on its back, belly exposed.

WITH ERECT EARS AND A PERKY TAIL, THIS DOG IS CONFIDENT AND ALERT.

THIS POINTER IS POISED FOR ACTION, WITH WEIGHT LEANING FORWARD AND TAIL EXTENDED.

PERSISTENTLY AGGRESSIVE DOGS SHOULD BE MUZZLED WHEN THEY ARE IN PUBLIC TO AVOID DANGEROUS FIGHTS.

A number of ritual forms of behaviour are common to all dogs, particularly during courtship and among dogs at play. Mating rituals are usually triggered by the scent of the female and advance with the male trying to attract the female's attention by leaping around. If he is successful, the dogs will first spar with their front legs before the female will allow the male to mount her. Dogs play as much as humans, perhaps to rehearse situations and to provide exercise. An invitation to play begins with the "play bow," when one dog drops on to its forelimbs, with its hindquarters raised, showing that it is about to play rather than engage in full combat. This is followed by tail-wagging and small leaps, with the mouth open, until the "opponent" takes up the chase, which usually ends with a mock fight. Some younger dogs can become overexcited, and owners must try to ensure that the games do not spiral out of control.

Given the highly efficient canine sense of smell, it is not surprising that scent is an important factor in dog behaviour. When two dogs meet, they immediately sniff each other's muzzle, inguinal, and anal areas to establish sex and status. Pheromones, present in saliva, urine, faeces, and vaginal and preputial secretions, provide a wealth of information to other dogs about the reproductive state of females and the dominance of males. Scent-marking — usually by urinating — is used by male dogs to establish territory and to communicate with other dogs.

A male dog may mark as many as eighty distinct sites with his urine within a four-hour period, and urban dogs who share their territory with many other animals mark more frequently than rural dogs. Female dogs also scent-mark, although their behaviour is more cyclical and restricted to one phase of the oestrous cycle. The urine of a female dog is extremely attractive to male dogs during her receptive phase. Dogs persistently sniff the ground when being walked, probably to ascertain which of their canine neighbours has preceded them.

Dogs also communicate vocally (although the basenji, a hunting dog from Central Africa, has no bark, it emits a yodel-like cry when it is happy). Canine hearing is well developed and dogs can hear sounds at much higher frequencies than humans. There are four main groups of canine sound, each with distinct meanings and uses: barking, howling, growling, and whining. Barking is the sound most commonly associated with dogs, and usually indicates excitement and a state of alertness; it is used as a warning signal if a dog's territory is being threatened. Howling is less common, but is the noise of pack animals. A communal sound, once one dog starts, its howling is quickly copied by other dogs within earshot. Growling dogs are obviously aggressive and on the verge of attacking or fighting, whereas whining or whimpering dogs are crying for attention. Puppies whimper as a sign of distress, while adult dogs do it to invoke sympathy. Interestingly, dogs rarely whine in the presence of other dogs unless they are trying to appease a dominant dog.

canine body language

MOOD	EARS	EYES	MOUTH/TEETH
Aggresive.	Close to head.	Staring fiorcefully.	Teeth bared in snarl.
Alert.	Erect. Moving to catch sounds.	Open normally.	Closed or slightly open, with teeth covered.
Anxious.	Slightly laid back.	Narrowed, avoiding gaze.	Closed – possibly in submissive 'grin.'.
Exerting dominance.	Erect or forward.	Staring at subject.	Closed.
Beginning of chase.	Upright.	Wide open and alert.	Open, possibly panting.
Excited.	Erect, pointing forwards.	Wide open.	Open, possibly panting.
Playful.	Erect or relaxed.	Wide open.	Relaxed, slight panting.
Submissive.	Down, laid against head.	Whites showing or narrowed.	Lips pulled back in 'submissive grin'.

BODY	TAIL	NOISE
Tense, dominant position. Poised for action.	Held straight out from body.	Growl or loud bark.
Slightly dominant position, possibly on tiptoes.	Up. Maybe wagging.	None. Possibly a low bark.
Tense, forelegs lowered.	Down. In submissive position.	Low whine or pleading bark.
Tall posture. Hackles up.	Stiffened.	Assertive growl.
Tense. Crouched, legs bent ready to run.	Extended straight out from body.	None.
Well balanced pose, possibly pacing or wriggling.	Wagging.	Short yelps of excitement.
'Play bow' – forelegs bent, rear raised. Possibly circling round, running to and fro.	Vigorous wagging.	Excited barking, play-growling.
Lying on back, belly exposed, one paw raised.	Between legs.	Whimper or low whine.

main dog types

Breed-specific traits have been developed over many generations of selective breeding, and dogs are now grouped according to the work for which they were bred. There are six groups of dogs in Britain: hound, gundog (sporting), terrier, utility (nonsporting), working, and toy. Dogs are divided into seven groups in the United States by the American Kennel Club (A.K.C.): sporting, nonsporting, hounds, terriers, toy, working, and herding. It is not always easy to classify a particular breed, and kennel clubs in different countries vary in their classifications. Most of the breeds that are popular today in the USA. and Britain emerged only within the last two-hundred to two-hundred-and-fifty years, with a great many being bred during the nineteenth century.

Dogs were once bred for guarding, herding, and hunting, utilizing characteristics that had evolved through natural selection. The Victorians were the first seriously to breed dogs for their looks alone, and during the nineteenth century kennel clubs began to lay down stringent rules governing the appearance of each breed. The genetic make-up of some breeds became governed by the whims of fashion, and some developed distorted features, such as massive heads, folded skin, or short, squashed muzzles. Traits that had been maintained in some breeds through natural selection over generations were subordinated to the demands of dog-show judges, and some breeds continue to suffer from damaging recessive genes that are detrimental to their health. Bulldogs, for example, are prized for their large heads and narrow hips, but their physique means that many litters must be delivered by Caesarean section. Dalmatians suffer from deafness, King Charles spaniels are prone to heart trouble, while German shepherds are susceptible to hip problems. Veterinary science and breeders are making good progress in their efforts to minimize these problems, however.

BASSET HOUND

MALTESE TOY.

BEAGLE.

DANDIE DINMONT.

BORZOI.

PEMBROKE CORGI.

AMERICAN COCKER SPANIEL.

FRENCH BULLDOG.

DOG GROUPS

Hounds are hunting dogs and can be divided into two categories: sight-hounds (also known as gaze-hounds) and scent-hounds. Greyhounds, Salukis, whippets, and borzois primarily use their sight to hunt, whereas beagles or bloodhounds hunt by following the scent of their prey. Aloof and independent, hounds generally concentrate on the world around them – the hunt – and can be deaf to the commands of their owners, so they maybe tricky dogs to train well. However, they adapt easily to family life and make excellent companions.

CHOW-CHOW.

Sporting gundogs excel at catching game, either birds or small, furry creatures. This group encompasses the setters and pointers that show huntsmen where the game is; the retrievers, which, as their name suggests, collect the dead game from either water or land; and the versatile spaniels that can do either job. Gundogs are adventurous, kindly animals and generally make good family pets.

KING CHARLES SPANIEL.

Terriers were bred to trap rodents, and this group encompasses a wide variety of dogs that are generally extremely active and lively from puppyhood. Long-legged terriers include breeds over 14 in (35 cm) high at the withers, while short-legged terriers measure less than 14 in (35 cm). Bull terriers are fearless, muscular dogs, and special terriers include such breeds as the Dandie Dinmont and the attractive and friendly West Highland terrier.

The working group includes the much-maligned Rottweiler, the massive Newfoundland, and the Pembroke corgi, a favorite at Buckingham Palace. Another diverse group, working breeds are further subdivided into guard and working dogs, herding and

MINIATURE PINSCHER.

shepherding dogs. Many breeds require particularly rigorous training to ensure their good behaviour, but they are level-headed dogs, with businesslike dispositions.

Utility breeds (known as the nonsporting group in the USA) are a diverse group, although they are all generally good companion dogs. Their sizes and body shape range from the small chow-chow through Dalmatians and poodles to Tibetan breeds and bulldogs, such as the French bulldog, which was once used for bull-baiting.

Dogs in the toy group are not among the largest breeds, but have big characters. Dogs such as the Chihuahua and Yorkshire terrier are undoubtedly brave; others, such as the King Charles spaniel, make excellent pets; and as a group they are generally intelligent dogs. They have been bred to be companion dogs and thrive on affection. Many, such as the "min pin," or miniature pinscher, are miniature versions of working dogs.

Critics of pedigree dogs believe that mongrels are healthier, more intelligent, and easier to train than their purebred cousins, but pedigree animals are infinitely more predictable in their behaviour. Although breeding to accentuate useful natural characteristics is no bad thing in a domestic animal, it is surely cruel to breed simply to accentuate physical characteristics that are momentarily deemed attractive, but that may actually make the animal's life miserable.

THE WEIMARANER IS A HANDSOME GUNDOG.

BICHON FRISE.

THREE

owning a dog

DOGS QUICKLY BECOME MUCH-LOVED MEMBERS OF THE FAMILY.

Choosing to become a dog-owner is not a decision to be made lightly, on impulse, or under pressure from persistent small children. A dog will be an addition to your family, a creature that will require care and attention for many years (the average life span for a dog is thirteen years). A potential dog-owner must consider whether he or she has the time and patience necessary to invest in a dog that will require feeding, grooming, walking, and stimulation. However, if you think that you can undertake this role, your time and effort

ALL DOGS NEED TO LEARN OBEDIENCE.

will be repaid handsomely by the affection of a faithful friend, who will give you years of pleasure, fun, and companionship. Above all, dogs are rewarding pets.

Before acquiring a dog, consider carefully what you want. Do you want to train a puppy? Or would you rather acquire a mature dog from a rescue home? Can you provide a regular routine for your pet? Do you have time to exercise it and play with it? If you are away at work all day, or would regularly leave your dog for longer than four hours, a dog is probably not the ideal pet for you because dogs are social creatures that dislike solitude. Do not forget the cost of owning a dog – in addition to food, it will require a collar, tag, vaccinations, veterinary treatment, and kennelling. Generally, large dogs cost more to maintain than small dogs.

FRIENDLY ANIMALS WILL WELCOME THEIR OWNERS.

Dogs have individual temperaments, but each breed exhibits certain general characteristics. By examining your lifestyle, you may be able to narrow down the sort of dog that will be right for you.

If you are usually inactive, and lack the time, ability, or inclination to exercise, consider a relatively sedentary breed that will be content with a short walk around the streets or to lie in its basket. A dog from the toy group, such as a Yorkshire terrier or a King Charles spaniel, would be ideal.

If you fancy a daily walk of about an hour, but preferably only in fine weather, you'll need an adaptable, easy-going breed, such as a terrier or a Shetland sheepdog. A large number of breeds would be suitable.

A dedicated walker, who delights in exercise whatever the weather, would appreciate an active dog – a gundog or working dog, such as a golden retriever, a bearded collie, or a boxer, for example. It is worth mentioning that these dogs also require mental stimulation because they are highly intelligent animals; obedience classes or agility training will be useful and can help to prevent behavioural problems.

If you have an outdoor lifestyle and would like a dog to be with you all day, choose a dog who thrives on this way of life, such as a Siberian husky, a Dalmatian, a pointer, or a retriever.

Families with children need a dog who will accept the rough and tumble of family life. Children must be taught how to treat a dog with respect, and a good

VETERINARY CARE IS A VITAL PART OF A DOG'S LIFE.

SMALL AND COMPACT, YORKSHIRE TERRIERS REQUIRE CONSIDERABLE GROOMING.

INTELLIGENT BEARDED COLLIES ENJOY TRAINING.

FIERCELY PROTECTIVE, KERRY BLUE TERRIERS ARE GOOD WITH CHILDREN.

ENERGETIC DALMATIANS NEED A LOT OF EXERCISE.

family dog must be easy-going, love exercise, and revel in attention. Gundogs, particularly Labradors, are popular family pets for precisely these reasons. A successful family dog must have been around children from puppyhood, so check the background of any animal that you may acquire from a rescue centre carefully. However gentle the dog, young children should never be left alone with it – small children are unpredictable creatures, as are even the most well-balanced dogs. (See also Chapter 5, page 108-145.)

Many academic studies have shown that pet-ownership is beneficial for both children and their families. Dogs act as a source of play and learning, and children will also learn the importance of responsibilities to animals, as well as the facts of life and, because dogs have comparatively short lives, how to cope with death, too. One study at Vienna University found that dog-owning children were likely to be more popular at school, possibly because they were learning about nonverbal communication through playing with their dogs.

CHILDREN SHOULD BE TAUGHT TO RESPECT AND ENJOY DOGS AND NOT TO MISTREAT OR BULLY THEM.

large or small?

The decision as to the best size of dog for you depends largely on your domestic circumstances. Put simply, do you have the room to accommodate a large animal, or is your home better suited to a small pet, such as spaniel? Large dogs are probably more costly to keep because they require more food, although small dogs are often picky eaters that demand specialized food.

Small dogs need almost as much exercise as their larger cousins, but do not require quite so much space in which to run around. Terriers, for example, must have regular exercise, whereas larger breeds, such as Irish wolfhounds, are more relaxed about the frequency of their exercise.

Large breeds with long-haired coats will drop hair around the house and will need frequent grooming, whereas dogs with nonshedding coats, such as poodles, would suit people with allergies. Long-haired breeds require the investment of a certain amount of time, dedication, and money to ensure that they look good.

LONG-HAIRED SPANIELS NEED DAILY GROOMING.

THE SHIH-TZU IS AN IDEAL PET FOR A SMALL HOME.

Crossbreeds often make the best family pets. They can be friendly, healthier, and longer-living than purebreeds and do not usually suffer from the painful congenital diseases that afflict many purebreeds. Mongrels are also more often in need of a good home than purebred dogs. On the other hand, pedigree dogs are known quantities: their behaviour is likely to conform to the expectations of the breed and their life expectancy is reasonably certain, as are any health problems.

Dogs vary widely in size and temperament, and it is important to match your individual needs to a suitable dog. Ask friends for recommendations, research the qualities of different breeds through books, magazines, or the Internet, and do not hurry your decision. Once you have chosen a breed, try to meet dogs of that breed of both sexes and all ages to gain an idea of what to expect at different stages in the dog's life.

adult or puppy?

It is vital to ascertain why an adult dog is being advertised. (Rescue centres, see page 77, will usually be able to furnish you with details of the dog's life and behaviour.) Be wary of a dog that has been rehomed several times: it may simply have been unlucky in its owners or it could have severe behavioural problems. Some – but not all – problems can be solved with a little patience. A dog with a destructive reputation may simply have been suffering from boredom, loneliness, and lack of exercise, for example.

Adult dogs typically arrive fully house-trained, which is a big advantage, but may suffer from a number of hidden problems, such as separation anxiety or a dislike of children. Carry out a few simple tests on the dog that you are considering. Watch its reaction when you put a lead on it and take it for a walk. How does it react to strangers, other dogs, and children? Is it easily frightened? Will it obey simple commands, such as "Sit"? Leave it alone to play with a toy for a few minutes.

BAD BEHAVIOUR OFTEN RESULTS FROM POOR CARE.

A dog that is prone to separation anxiety will bark or whine. Approach the dog from the front and maintain eye contact with it. A relaxed dog will watch you expectantly, but a nervous dog may bark or cower. While the dog is on a loose lead, stoke under its chin and along its back while talking quietly to it. A dog that fears hands (and therefore human contact) will pull away.

Puppies are infinitely lovable, but the small, cuddly, eight-week-old bundle will be an entirely different dog in six months' time. To state the obvious, puppies grow, sometimes to very large proportions, and a large dog may not only be less appealing, but will require a lot of space and will be expensive to feed. Try to view the parents if possible, if only to gain an idea of the size that your puppy will eventually reach. Puppies will be quite labour-intensive for the first few months, and their owners must be prepared to devote time and patience to them.

It is quite hard to determine the character of a puppy when it is only a few weeks old, but even in a young litter, some individuals will be shy and others nosy and adventurous, so use these guidelines to select the kind of dog you want.

MALE OR FEMALE?

In general terms, male dogs from dominant breeds are more likely to roam and to be more aggressive than females. They will probably be more active, playful, and little more difficult to train, too. Females are generally more placid, gentle, and easier to train, but may demand more affection. (Note that females have two menstrual cycles per year, when they emit blood-tinged discharges.) Among small and more submissive breeds, temperamental differences between the sexes are less marked.

SPEND TIME ASSESSING HOW AN ADULT DOG INTERACTS WITH PEOPLE AND RESPONDS TO SIMPLE COMMANDS.

Points to consider when choosing a dog

- Large or small?
- Puppy or adult?
- Pedigree or crossbreed?
- The size of your house.
- Your lifestyle – are you out at work all day?
- How much exercise are you prepared
  to provide?
- The background of an adult dog.

PUPPIES NEED PLENTY OF CARE.

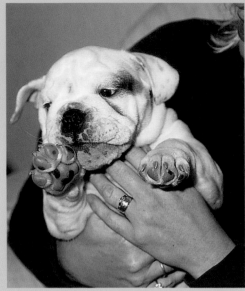

CAREFULLY CHECK A POTENTIAL PET.

adopting a dog

BREEDERS

Once you have decided on the breed of dog that is best suited to your situation, you'll have to decide where to get it from. Reputable breeders are probably the best source for pedigree animals, although these dogs will be more expensive than crossbreeds or rescue dogs. In Britain, breed-club details can be found by contacting the Kennel Club.

Dog-breeding is a specialized discipline, and good breeders choose their blood stock carefully and ensure that their animals have an excellent quality of life. They will never breed from an animal that is likely to pass on inherited medical problems, nor will they breed from a bitch under two years of age or over eight. Breeding bitches usually produce no more than three or four litters during their lifetime and are never mated in two consecutive seasons. (It is now illegal in Britain for breeders to mate a bitch before she is a year old, to allow a bitch to have more than six litters in a lifetime, or to allow her to produce more than one litter a year.)

Breeders do not sell their dogs to pet stores, dealers, or other commercial outlets. They should be knowledgeable about their breed and frank about the disadvantages of their dogs. They should be equally keen to learn about your circumstances. Good breeders will also offer to take a puppy back should your domestic circumstances change.

Be prepared to put your name on a waiting list for a puppy – a well-bred puppy from a good breeder is worth waiting for. Once the litter has been born, visit it to watch the puppies interacting with the mother and ask to see the father if possible. Check that the puppies have regular human contact, preferably with

more than one person, that the facilities are clean, and that the puppies appear alert and healthy. Choose a puppy that is interested in its surroundings rather than one that hides in the background (but be aware that such a puppy may develop into a dominant dog). The puppy should be confident, mischievous, appealing, and curious.

Once you have chosen a puppy, you will probably be asked to pay a deposit. Ensure that the breeder has prepared the relevant paperwork, which should include pedigree and registration papers, as well as the parents' hereditary screening certificates. Ask for a written agreement that the purchase is dependent on

REPUTABLE BREEDERS CAN PROVIDE HEALTHY DOGS.

a satisfactory examination by a vet within forty-eight hours of the purchase. Find out whether the puppy has been wormed and vaccinated (some breeders do this at eight weeks before releasing puppies to new homes).

On the day of collection, check that the puppy is healthy, with no sores, scabs, discharges from the nose or eyes, any kind of cough, or other signs of illness. If the puppy appears poorly, do not take it, but arrange to pick it up on another day. Arrange to have your puppy examined by a vet on the day of collection, too. You and your family will bond strongly with the animal within twenty-four hours, and if the vet decides that it should be returned to the breeder for any reason, parting with it will be much harder once you have become attached to it.

COLLECT VITAL PAPERWORK FROM THE BREEDER.

RESCUE CENTRES AND OTHER SOURCES

Rescue or rehoming centres house animals that have been surrendered by their owners for a variety of reasons. Many people, for example, have simply acquired the wrong dog for their circumstances and are unable to look after it adequately, while other animals arrive as a result of domestic upheaval, and still more are the product of an unexpected litter of puppies.

Rehoming centres are committed to the welfare of dogs and are keen to prevent any further distress to their animals. They often make behavioural assessments of their dogs and carry out medical tests and neutering programmes. Such centres question prospective owners closely about their lifestyle, accommodation, family circumstances, and their expectations of dog-ownership.

Some especially rigorous organizations even arrange for a pre-adoption talk or ask for a reference from a vet.

MANY UNWANTED PUPS END UP IN RESCUE CENTRES.

The dogs available from rescue centres are mainly crossbreeds, but there are a number of specialist-breed rescue societies, too. If you are considering taking a puppy from a rescue centres, it is vital to visit it and see it with its mother first. A well-adjusted puppy will play and socialize with its littermates and will benefit from its mother's care. (If you are tempted to buy a puppy advertised in a newspaper, you may not have the opportunity to assess its background, and if the puppy has been badly cared for, it could grow into an aggressive, troublesome dog with behavioural problems.)

Dog-owning friends are another good source, and you will usually be able to visit the mother, and possibly also the father, of your prospective dog. Local vets may be helpful, too, and if a dog is

recommended, it is likely that the vet will know the animal's medical and behavioural background.

Dogs sold by pet shops are prone to diseases and behavioural problems created during the vital early months of a puppy's life because it may have suffered periods of isolation and inadequate contact with people.

HEALTH CHECK

Before purchasing a dog, make a few basic checks to ascertain the state of its health. This is especially important with puppies.

Watch the whole litter of puppies running about in a small space; they are likely to empty their bladders and bowels, giving you the chance to check that their motions are reasonably formed, with no sign of diarrhoea. A puppy that does not join in the romping may be tired, lame, or simply unsociable.

You should be able to pick up a puppy without it whimpering or showing signs of distress as you examine its body. Puppies must be held carefully in the crook of the arm (rather as you would hold a baby), with one hand supporting the hindquarters and the base of the spine and the other the forelimbs and head.

Anyone selling an adult dog should be able to supply details of its medical history and vaccinations.

A RELAXED DOG WITH ITS NEW OWNER.

Look over the puppy's body, checking the following points.

- Skin: depending on the breed, the skin should have loose folds.
- Coat: should be clean and shiny.
- Tail root: check for fleas.
- Anal area: should be clean.
- Belly: should be supple and reasonably flat.
- Ears: check the edges for lice.
- Nose: should be cool and moist, with no discharge.
- Eyes: should be open and bright.

preparing your home for the arrival of your dog

A HIGH, STURDY FENCE KEEPS DOGS SAFE.

OUTDOOR AND INDOOR SECURITY

Before bringing your new dog home, make sure that your house and garden are secure and that the dog will not be able to escape into the road either by digging or leaping. Garden fences and gates must be secured, pools and ponds covered, and poisonous pesticides stored out of reach (and in some cases not used at all).

Try to look at your garden through a dog's eyes and to see any potential hazards from a dog's eye level. It may be necessary to insert paving stones around your garden fence to prevent it from digging and burrowing. Check the whole garden for holes and gaps, which are especially attractive to puppies, which have tendency to explore every nook and cranny without giving any thought to how they might get out of small cracks and crevices. High-sided ponds are another potential hazard for puppies, which, if they fell in, would find it difficult to climb out of again. If your dog turns out to be a persistent digger, consider converting a corner of the garden into a sandpit where it can bury its toys. Instead of punishing it for digging elsewhere, reward it with a treat every time that it digs in the sandpit.

Inside, carry out the same checks that you would make before the arrival of a toddler. Tidy away all trailing electrical wires, stabilize fragile furniture, and, if necessary, remove treasured ornaments until the new dog or puppy has settled in. Place any toxic houseplants well out of the dog's reach, too. In the case of a puppy, remove anything that looks

THIS CAGE OR CRATE PROVIDES A SECURE HOME.

CHECK THAT YOUR DOG CANNOT DIG UNDER FENCES.

ENSURE THAT GARDEN HAZARDS LIKE THIS POND ARE ADEQUATELY FENCED TO AVOID ACCIDENTS.

remotely chewable, such as shoes, gloves, children's toys, and even the post on the doormat. Give the dog three chewable toys of different textures and never leave a dog that likes chewing alone in a room that contains live electric wires.

INTRODUCING A DOG TO OTHER PETS

Contrary to the image projected in cartoons, dogs and cats are not natural enemies and will happily coexist if properly introduced. Try to ensure that the cat does not run away from the dog while they are being introduced – and restrain the dog – because this will simply induce the dog to chase the cat. It will then try to frighten the cat into running away each time that they subsequently meet simply for the fun of it, which will not make for a peaceful household. It may be worth putting the cat into a basket or cage for the first meeting, which will allow the dog to sniff it and satisfy its curiosity without making mischief.

Many owners fail to realize how much a single dog (rather like an only child) can miss the fun and companionship provided by another dog. Once a dog slows down in middle age, the introduction of another

MANY DOGS AND CATS COEXIST HAPPILY.

YOUNG DOGS CAN LEARN FROM OLDER ANIMALS.

dog to the household may perk it up. Introduce them on neutral ground, away from sleeping or feeding areas. Never give either dog preferential treatment and do not leave the two dogs alone together until they have established a good relationship.

POINTS FOR CONSIDERATE DOG-OWNERSHIP

- Never let your dog foul the pavement – make it defecate in the gutter, "scoop the poop," and dispose of it either in a toilet or a specially provided bin. At home, encourage your dog to use one corner of the garden so that you do not always have to watch where you're walking.

- Although parks and beaches are excellent open spaces for exercising dogs, try to retain a degree of control over your dog. Some parents are nervous of dogs near children's play areas and few people appreciate being showered with water as a wet dog races past them on a beach.

- Never take your dog for a walk without a lead. If traffic is visible, even at a distance, it is simply too dangerous to allow a dog to run free: if something catches its eye, it may run off into the path of on-coming vehicles. Even in woodland areas, where dogs can run freely, it may either encounter horse-riders or small children or may disappear to chase rabbits, making a lead useful for control.

- Carry some doggy treats with which to bribe your dog. Give it one before letting it off the lead and another as a reward when it returns when called.

- Never leave your dog in an unventilated car.

- Remember that not everyone shares your love of your dog. Some people are genuinely scared of dogs, for a variety of reasons, and although their behaviour may appear irrational, the considerate dog-owner will respect their feelings.

equipment

Although there is a huge variety of equipment available with which to pamper dogs of all shapes, sizes, and ages, the basic equipment needed to make your dog comfortable and safe is quite limited. At the very least, a dog needs a collar and lead, a comfortable sleeping area, a few items of grooming equipment, and food and water bowls.

COLLARS, TAGS, LEADS, AND HARNESSES

Collars are available in leather, nylon, or cotton in a range of styles and prices. Simple buckle collars suit many dogs, but a halfcheck collar with a "choke chain" may be more suitable for restraining energetic animals. Rolled-leather collars make a smaller indentation in a dog's coat than flat collars.

A puppy's first collar should be lightweight and inexpensive (it will soon outgrow it). When fitting a collar, ensure that it is loose enough to allow you to slip at least two fingers underneath it and that it will not slip over the puppy's head when it pulls back against it. Allow a puppy gradually to grow accustomed to wearing its collar by fitting it for an hour or two at a time.

AN ELECTRONIC TAG.

In Britain, dog-owners are legally obliged to attach some form of identification to their dogs, so either fit an identity tag engraved with your address or telephone number to its collar or have your dog microchipped, a relatively new method of labelling dogs that must be carried out by a vet. Microchipping is an easy process, no more painful than a vaccination, in which a microchip, the size of a grain of rice (encased in biocompatible glass to prevent rejection by the dog's body), is implanted in the loose fold of skin on the back of a dog's neck. The chip carries a number unique to the dog, which is stored on a national database and refers to information about the dog and its vaccinations, its owner, and address. The microchip is read by a scanner that uses low-frequency waves to activate it.

A BASIC ENGRAVED IDENTITY TAG.

It is imperative that you maintain control over your dog, particularly in public places, so once your dog is used to wearing a collar, attach a lightweight lead to it before taking it for walks. You will probably need a short lead, about (6 ft) (2 m) in length; a long training lead, about 20 ft (6 m) in length, made of cotton or meshed nylon; and a long houseline for use at home.

PRACTICE BASIC OBEDIENCE LESSONS AT HOME.

LEATHER LEADS ARE HARD-WEARING.

LONGER LEASHS ARE USEFUL DURING TRAINING.

MICROCHIPPING IS A PAINLESS PROCEDURE.

Some boisterous dogs, or breeds with especially fragile windpipes, such as Yorkshire terriers, may need a body harness or halter instead of a lead. Head halters are similar to those used on horses and enable you to exert a little more control over energetic large dogs (when the dog runs off, pressure is applied to the halter, which pulls the head down). Ask your vet for advice if you are unsure about the best lead for your dog.

BEDDING

All dogs appreciate a place of their own, where they feel secure. It must be away from draughts and provide sufficient warmth for the dog (obviously, long-haired breed are better insulated than short-coated ones). A moulded-plastic dog bed lined with a small doggy mattress will provide both the security of "walls" to lie against and the comfort of a soft surface. Your dog's bedding needs to be washable and comfortable. As well as being washable, synthetic, fake-fur material is warm, and dogs appear to love snuggling into it. Bean-bag beds, another popular style, are well insulated, mould themselves to the dog's body, and are exceptionally snug. Wicker baskets, which were once popular, are, however, both difficult to clean and, particularly in the case of puppies, eminently chewable.

Puppies' beds can be temporary affairs, but must be either disposable or easy to clean. A cardboard box with a piece cut out of the front and lined with newspaper and an old blanket is adequate to start with. As the puppy grows, it can graduate to a proper bed.

If you intend to keep your dog outside, you will need to provide it with a secure, weatherproof outbuilding furnished with a comfortable bed. (If it has a concrete floor, make sure that the bed is raised.) The kennel (or shed) must have ventilation and light provided by a window so that it will not become too hot in warm

BEDS CAN BE MADE FROM SIMPLE CARDBOARD BOXES.

caring for your dog

DOGS APPRECIATE THEIR OWN SPACE.

OUTDOOR DOG KENNELS MUST BE SNUG AND DRY.

BEDS MUST BE PLACED AWAY FROM DRAUGHTS.

weather. Purpose-built kennels with runs attached are another option; usually constructed of wood, these are easy to scrub down and keep clean.

GROOMING EQUIPMENT

All dogs need regular grooming, but it clearly takes longer to maintain the coats of long-haired breeds. Although it is important to train your dog to sit still during grooming sessions, most dogs accept – and even enjoy – basic grooming, which consists of brushing the coat, cleaning the face, and checking the nails (which should be trimmed with special nailclippers for dogs).

There is a wide variety of grooming equipment on sale to suit every type of coat, and your choice should depend on your dog's coat, although every dog-owner will need a brush and comb. Short-haired dogs, such as boxers, require a hard brush that massages the skin while removing loose hair, but this would be entirely unsuitable on the long coat of a rough collie, for example. A rubber brush and a chamois cloth are also useful, the latter for "polishing" the coat to produce a healthy shine. Fine-haired dogs, such as Yorkshire terriers, must be brushed with a soft pin brush and a wide-toothed comb, while breeds

with thick coats, such as sheepdogs, require brisk brushing with a soft pin brush, a comb, and a firm bristle brush. Long-haired dogs can be groomed with a "slicker" brush to tease out tangles; a bristle brush to enhance the coat's shine; a comb to part the coat neatly and to comb the legs; and scissors to trim the hair around the paws. Trimmed breeds, such as poodles, will need trimming every two months or so with electric clippers, which must be sharpened regularly by a professional service. A breeder or vet will be able to advise on the most suitable grooming equipment for your pet.

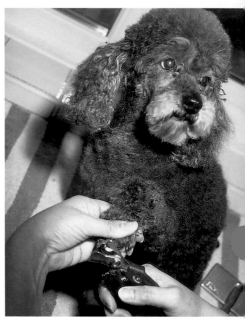

NAIL-CLIPPING IS PART OF REGULAR GROOMING.

FOOD BOWLS

Dogs should have their own food and water bowls, which must be kept apart from human utensils. Although dogs are perfectly clean, a number of zoonotic diseases can be passed from animals to humans through poor hygiene. For the same reason, it is sensible to dedicate a special tin-opener, spoon, and fork to dog-food preparation.

Dogs' appetites vary according to the size of the animal: big breeds have hearty appetites, for instance, in which case buy large food and water bowls. Available in metal, plastic, or ceramic designs, bowls must be robust, easy to clean, hard to tip over, unattractive to dogs that like chewing, and reasonably

heavy so that the dog cannot pick them up. If you have more than one dog, each must have its own food bowl. Place the bowls on a mat to absorb any spills.

Clean the food bowl after each meal and replenish the water bowl at least once a day.

TOYS

Dogs are naturally inclined to pull, chase, and tug things, and puppies are especially keen on chewing, so if you want to avoid your home and possessions being damaged, invest in a few toys.

CHEWY TOYS ARE POPULAR WITH DOGS OF ALL AGES.

Make sure that toys are well made and too large to be swallowed. Rubber and rope tug toys are ideal for indoors, while Frisbees, soft rubber balls, and throw toys on a rope make good outdoor toys. Dogs also enjoy bone-shaped chewies or squeaky toys (although the sound of these may either irritate you or over-excite your dog).

travel

Dogs often have to travel with their owners in cars, be it to a park for exercise, to the vet, or on longer trips. Some dogs become very excited by motorized travel and will bark, leap around, or pace, behaviour that is neither safe nor peaceful in a confined space. Although most dogs experience no ill effects during such journeys, there are a number of ways of both improving your dog's safety and making the trip more comfortable for it.

Try to accustom your dog to travelling by car from an early age. Young puppies are often sick, a problem that they usually grow out of. Do not feed a dog immediately before motorized travel. Before beginning a long journey, exercise your dog; it is also advisable to stop every two hours to allow the dog to have a run, relieve itself, and have a drink.

Either put an old sheet or rug over the back seat or, if you have an estate car or hatchback, settle your dog at the rear of the vehicle (fit a metal grille to prevent the dog from leaping in to the seating area). A crate-trained dog will happily lie securely in its crate for journeys of any length; not only is this probably the most secure method of transporting a dog, but, in the event of an accident, it will ensure that the dog will not be flung around the car. Another alternative is to train your dog to sit in a purpose-built, moulded travel container secured within the vehicle.

A GRILLE PREVENTS DOGS FROM LEAPING AROUND.

ENSURE THAT YOUR DOG IS SECURE IN YOUR VEHICLE.

KENNELS CARE FOR DOGS WHOSE OWNERS ARE AWAY.

A PET CARRIER IS USEFUL TO TRANSPORT PUPPIES.

MOST DOGS IN KENNELS ARE VERY WELL CARED FOR.

In hot weather, make sure that your car is well ventilated and carry a flask of water and a bowl so that your dog can have a drink. Try not to leave your dog alone in your car, but if you really must, ensure that it is well ventilated and park in the shade if possible. Never leave your dog in an car without opening the windows slightly: dogs have poor control of their body temperature and can easily become overheated, often fatally so. If the weather is really hot, leave the dog at home, where it will be more comfortable.

Holidays

Before acquiring a dog, think about what you will do when you go away on holiday. Do you have a friend living nearby who could accommodate your pet? If not, consider kennels as an alternative. Ask dog-owning friends for their recommendations or get a list of local kennels from your vet.

All good kennels should be open for inspection. Check that the dogs are exercised and appear well groomed and try to chat to the staff – enthusiastic employees are a sign of a good kennels. The kennels staff should ask to see vaccination certificates to guard against the introduction of disease, and will also need information about your dog's diet, medication, and infirmities. Prices vary according to the facilities; at the very least, kennels should provide secure, weatherproof accommodation and adequate food. It is advisable to book well in advance of popular holiday periods.

Boarding can be upsetting for a dog, especially one with a strong attachment to its owner, so the younger a dog starts boarding, the better, because it will learn that the stay in kennels is only temporary. If you do your research properly, you will be able to leave your dog secure in the knowledge that it will be well cared for in your absence.

However, you may prefer to hire a dog-sitter to care for it in your home. Vets can usually provide a list of reputable house and dog-sitting services.

FOUR

puppies

Irresistibly cute, furry bundles of fun and mischief – and lots of hard work – puppies

are especially appealing. Hard-boiled individuals who would never consider pet-

ownership often find themselves bowled over by a desire to look after these little

PUPPIES ARE FUN, UNDENIABLY CUTE. . .AND A LOT OF HARD WORK!

PUPPIES SPEND THEIR FIRST FEW WEEKS SIMPLY EATING AND SLEEPING.

creatures, and children persistently pester their parents for a furry playmate. The desire to protect small creatures is inherent in us all, but what happens when the cuddly ball of fur grows into a large, demanding dog? And how can you get it to obey your commands? Most importantly, just how long does it take to house-train your pooch?

the first weeks

For the first two weeks of life, puppies are completely dependent on their mother for warmth, food, and protection as their senses develop, their eyes open, and they gradually begin to respond to the world around them. During the next two weeks, puppies become a little more independent, wagging their tails, growling, barking, and starting to move away from their mother as their bodies become able to control their temperature more efficiently. They then begin a period of intense socialization, when they absorb smells, sights, sounds, touches, and experiences, all of which will help them in adult life. It is vital that puppies have human contact during these early weeks so that they grow accustomed to people. The wider a dog's experience as a puppy, the more adaptable it will be in later life.

Puppies are usually taken away from their mother between six and twelve weeks of age. This is inevitably a stressful time for a young dog, and it is important for new owners to establish a feeling of security and trust. Try to collect your new puppy in the morning so that it will have a day to explore its new home and get used to new faces, smells, and sounds before going to sleep. Arrange for two people to collect the puppy so that one can sit with it in the back of the car (and remember to protect the seat with an old towel or blanket in case it is sick).

bedding and bedtime

Having carried out the safety checks recommended on pages 80 to 82, introduce the puppy to its sleeping area. Until it is house-trained, it probably makes sense to house him in the kitchen, where spills and accidents are more easily cleared up. Because the kitchen is also likely to be warm, and full of welcoming smells, it provides a good introduction to a
new home.

Housing the puppy's bed within a playpen will enable it to have a secure place of its own, as well as preventing it from getting up to mischief. Puppies need a large amount of sleep, so it is important to provide a quiet site, away from the excitement of the household, where it can snooze after meals. Line its bed with newspaper to absorb the inevitable accidents.

THE WALLS OF THIS BED PROVIDE A FEELING OF SECURITY FOR YOUR DOG.

A MAT WILL PROVIDE A SOFT, DRAUGHT-FREE SURFACE.

PPIES MUST GET USED TO BEING HANDLED.

THIS BEAN-BAG-STYLE BED IS IDEAL FOR YOUNG DOGS AS IT IS WARM AND COZY — RATHER LIKE THEIR MOTHERS.

There are several theories about how to deal with new puppies at night. Like human babies, puppies are likely to wake up, when they'll find a human presence very comforting. However, they must become used to falling asleep alone, and it is never too early to start training. Your approach will probably depend on how strong-willed you are in the face of a small, upset dog.

One recommendation is to tuck it up snugly next to a ticking alarm clock, which simulates the beating of its mother's heart, before leaving it to sleep. A few whines are inevitable, but it should settle eventually. (Remember to cover the floor with newspaper and not to leave it for longer than six hours without taking it outside to relieve itself.)

Another school of thought, however, advocates putting the puppy's bed in the owner's bedroom for the first few nights in a new home. This will provide the security of knowing that a human presence is close, and also means that you will not have to trek down to the kitchen if you need to resettle the dog. If you opt for this approach, make sure that your puppy naps alone during the day and gradually extend this habit until it is spending the night alone in its designated sleeping area.

CRATE-TRAINING

Crates may appear to be little more than cages, but if a dog has been accustomed to one since it was a puppy, it will regard it as a secure place. Crates, which differ from playpens in that they cover a smaller area, should only be used for resting or sleeping. Do not leave a puppy in a crate for more than two hours during the day.

1 Place soft bedding, a bowl of water, and a toy inside the crate. Leave the door open, and your puppy will probably wander inside out of curiosity.

2 Show your puppy a treat, put the treat into the crate, and say "Go to your crate" to lure the puppy inside. Keep the door open.

3 Do not close the door until your puppy is used to being in the crate – this may take a couple of sessions.

4 Once your puppy appears happy inside its crate, take it outside for some exercise, then encourage it to return to its crate, where it will probably play quietly before falling asleep.

If your dog has been crate-trained, travel is made easier because you can use the crate in the car, thus providing your dog with a safe and secure travelling environment.

house-training

Dogs are clean animals who will try to avoid soiling their sleeping areas, and house-training is simply about encouraging them to relieve themselves in a place that is convenient to the owner. It is a process that requires perseverance and patience, but daytime habits can probably be established within a week.

Dogs often sniff the ground before urinating, or else circle rapidly, so watch out for these signs and then act quickly because there will only be seconds between warning and performance. Puppies usually want to urinate as soon as they wake up and after a meal, so prepare for this either by taking your puppy outside or putting it on some newspaper on awakening, after each meal, and last thing at night. Make sure that you provide regular opportunities for it to relieve itself throughout the day.

To encourage your puppy to use the same area again, keep a piece of soiled newspaper and put it underneath the top sheet of fresh newspaper. The puppy will recognize its own odour and quickly learn to use the same spot. If you take your puppy outside, take it to the same spot each time and encourage it with a command, such as "Be quick" or "Hurry up." Praise your puppy extravagantly when it has urinated in the correct place.

Never discipline a puppy when it has had an accident on the floor, nor rub its nose in the mess, because these actions will simply make it scared of you. If you see it urinating (or worse) indoors, say "No" very sternly, and then move it to your designated spot. Never play with your puppy outside until it has performed.

Dog faeces is both unpleasant and a health risk, so always clean up after your dog. Use a plastic bag or "pooper scooper" to clear up the mess and either dispose of it in a dog bin or flush it down the toilet.

TEACH PUPS TO ASK TO GO OUTSIDE – QUICKLY!

KEEP TEMPTING SHOES AWAY FROM YOUNG DOGS.

PUPPIES MUST BE TAUGHT TO GO TO SLEEP ALONE.

Clean up any accidents inside the house with disinfectant, but try to avoid products that smell of ammonia because this may remind the puppy of the smell of its own urine.

DRIED FOOD IS CONVENIENT AND DELICIOUS.

TREATS ARE USEFUL TO HELP TRAIN PUPPIES.

feeding

Breeders often supply the owners of new puppies with a diet sheet, and it is sensible to follow it closely. If you suddenly change a puppy's diet, it may result in an upset stomach, so if you want to make any changes, do so gradually and allow the puppy to adjust itself to the new food.

Puppies are usually weaned off their mother's milk by the age of five or six weeks. Once they can eat and drink on their own, they like to eat little and often; an eight-week-old dog should probably have four small meals each day. Adjust this amount over time, so that by six months your dog is on two meals a day, and on just one by the time it is a year old. (Naturally, the amount of food must be increased!) As they become bigger, puppies' lack of enthusiasm for first one, then another, feed becomes obvious, so the reduction in the number of meals is a natural progression. Some small dogs, or breeds with sensitive stomachs, such as borzois, thrive better on two or three small meals even as adults.

The nutritional requirements of growing puppies are considerable, and it is essential for the dog's general health that it receives a balanced diet. A good diet helps to realize the puppy's potential for growth and development; a diet that is in some way deficient may mean that a dog fails to reach the full physical potential of its breed.

ADJUST YOUR DOG'S DIET TO ACCOMMODATE HIS CHANGING NEEDS AS HE GROWS.

Dogs need protein, essential fatty acids, mineral elements, vitamins, and carbohydrates. Calcium is critical, but they do not need fruit or green vegetables because their bodies make plenty of vitamin C. Water is also, of course, essential, and every dog should have constant access to a clean bowl of water. Dog-food manufacturers produce special foods for puppies, whose calorie requirement is quiet high in comparison to their size. Consult your vet if you are unsure about any aspect of your pet's diet. (See 158 to 181 for more information about diets.)

Puppies are relentless chewers. Teething occurs around the ages of four to six months and again at six to eight months, when the adult teeth erupt; chewing helps this process, as well as providing a bit of relief from teething pain. Protect vulnerable items in your home either by removing them from sight or sprinkling pepper on items like electric flexes to discourage damage. Alternatively, buy a non-toxic, bitter-tasting spray from your vet or pet shop to spray on objects that you do not want to be chewed. Give your puppy a chewable toy to play with, such as a large rubber bone, but not an old slipper because it will not understand that other shoes and slippers are out of bounds. Make sure that your puppy understands what it can chew and what it must not touch, otherwise poor behavioural patterns will become established, which will be hard to break.

PROTECT YOUR HOME FROM A CHEWING PUPPY.

BEHAVIOUR AT FEEDING TIME

Dogs have a primitive instinct to guard their feeding bowls tenaciously, and are very competitive at meal times. Although such behaviour may seem sweet in a puppy, it is less amusing in an adult dog, so discourage it by deliberately approaching your puppy while it is

GIVE YOUNG DOGS ARTIFICIAL BONES TO CHEW.

feeding and then patting or moving its bowl slightly. Reward the puppy if it allows you to do this without complaint. As the puppy becomes used to this, it will understand that its food is safe and should become less defensive.

Dogs must also learn that they should eat after their owners and then only from their own bowls. This reinforces the fact that the owner is dominant and the "pack leader" in the household.

REAL BONES MAY SPLINTER INSIDE A DOG'S MOUTH, SO USE MANUFACTURED ONES LIKE THIS INSTEAD.

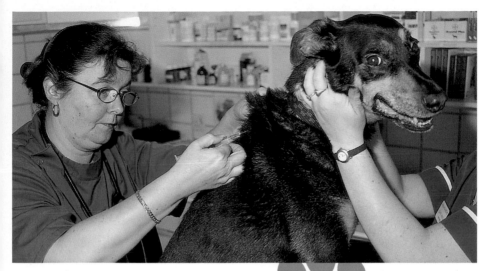

ALL DOGS MUST BE VACCINATED AGAINST COMMON CANINE ILLNESSES.

vaccinations

Until a puppy has completed its course of vaccinations, it is at risk of infection, both from other dogs and from infections that may be carried into the house on visitors' clothes. Restrict its outings until it is protected.

The vaccination regime varies from puppy to puppy, and is dependent on the level of immunity passed to the young dog through its mother's milk, as well as disease problems in a particular area. Your vet will advise you on the best course of action, but puppies are generally inoculated at eight weeks, twelve weeks, and eighteen weeks of age against distemper, hepatitis, parvovirus, and leptospirosis. The first combined vaccination is given at eight weeks and repeated at twelve weeks, when the first dose of parvovirus vaccine is administered, which is boosted at eighteen weeks.

Leptospirosis is a bacterial disease that affects the liver and kidneys, while parvovirus is a highly infectious, and often fatal, viral disease that affects the heart and bowel. Kennel-cough vaccine may also be administered at the first-stage vaccination. Booster injections are given at regular intervals throughout the dog's life, although the hepatitis vaccination confers life-long protection.

basic training and exercise

You should impose your rules upon a puppy as soon as it enters your household. It must learn the basics:

- to wear a collar and leash and obey the family
- to eat only from its own food bowl
- to sleep in its own bed
- to come when called
- to wait on command.

Choosing, and then using, a suitable name for your dog is an important part of a puppy's training. Pick a short, simple name and use it frequently when addressing your puppy.

A puppy understands only a few words and will respond more to tone of voice than to what is actually being said, so choose one word for a command and stick to it; do not, for example, alternate between "come" and "here" in recall training because this will confuse your dog. Speak softly to your dog – this forces it to listen hard to what you're saying. Use hand signals to reinforce your commands, especially outdoors.

Puppies are energetic creatures, but tire quickly. They obviously need less exercise than adult dogs; treat

COMMAND.

even large breeds with caution because they take longer to mature than smaller breeds and their legs and joints can be permanently damaged by too much exercise.

Because a puppy's attention span is limited, keep lessons short. Fifteen-minute sessions four times a day are probably enough for a young dog. Always praise your dog when it has obeyed a command.

Edible treats are also an excellent way of showing your puppy that you are pleased with it, but as you repeat the exercises, decrease the treats until it responds to your commands without being bribed. Most importantly, keep training sessions fun and be aware that because your puppy regards your training sessions as just another play activity, you'll need to be patient and keep your sense of humor. Always end a training session with a short period of play time.

ENCOURAGE.

REWARD.

Training a Young Dog to Wear a Collar and Lead

1 Let your puppy see and sniff the collar and lead while you are both indoors. Put the collar and lead on your puppy for short periods so that it becomes used to them. Never use a choke or check chain on a puppy: a sharp tug may frighten it and a loose chain may snag on an obstacle, strangling the dog.

2 Attach a lightweight lead to the collar, keep it slack, and begin walking while calling the puppy by name. If the dog sets off in another direction, go with it, keeping the lead slack and talking to it. The aim is accustom the puppy to the feel of the lead. After five or six lessons, when the puppy is used to wearing the collar and lead at home, take it for a short, fifteen-minute walk around the streets. Try to understand how overwhelming traffic, rushing people, and the attendant noise may be for your dog.

ALLOW PUPPIES TO SNIFF OTHER PETS.

New Experiences

To a young dog, the world outside the house is strange, frightening, and full of excitement, so you'll need to train it to deal with new experiences. To do this, train your puppy to understand simple commands in the house and introduce it to a variety of new experiences, such as meeting strangers and children, getting used to automobile journeys, playing with other animals, and developing road sense.

To accustom your puppy to meeting strangers, try to introduce it to someone who looks completely dissimilar to you – perhaps someone with a beard, someone wearing a hat, or someone carrying an unusual object. Let the puppy sniff this person until it realizes that although he or she may look different, the stranger is just another friendly human being. Arrange for such meetings to take place both indoors and outdoors so that the dog becomes used to the approach of strangers.

Make sure that whoever is meeting the dog bends down to the dog's level and perhaps offers a small treat as an incentive.

When you think that your dog is ready, start to teach it road sense. This is nothing less than a survival technique for dogs, who must learn to stop at kerbs. To a small dog, vehicles may appear very intimidating at first, but once it has become accustomed to the noises and smells, command it to sit every time that you come to a kerb. Your dog will soon learn to sit and wait for your command before crossing a road. Never let your dog off a leash in a busy urban area, however well-trained it may be.

FIVE

exercises & training

Dogs must be trained to teach them their place in life and their status within the family. Intelligent, untrained dogs will get into trouble, perhaps causing road accidents, worrying sheep, frightening strangers, and generally making themselves unpopular within the neighbourhood. Owners who do not train their dogs in the basics of good behaviour are irresponsible: badly behaved dogs should not be blamed for any mayhem that they may cause – it is the fault of their owners. British legislation reflects this, and dog-owners are obliged to control their pets wherever they are. The 1991 Dangerous Dogs Act states that it is a criminal offence to allow your dog to be out of control in a public place, including your car, and if anyone feels threatened by your dog (let alone actually attacked by it), they are within their rights to report you, as its owner, to the police. If you are found guilty under this act, your dog could be destroyed, and you could receive a prison sentence of six months and/or a £5,000 fine.

ENTHUSIASTIC DOGS SHOULD BE TAUGHT NOT TO JUMP UP AT STRANGERS.

EXERCISE SHOULD BE AN ENJOYABLE TIME FOR YOU AND YOUR DOG.

GIVE YOUR DOG A FEW TOYS TO STIMULATE IT.

DOGS LOVE PLAYING TOGETHER.

AGILITY TRAINING: CERTAIN BREEDS LOVE JUMPING THROUGH HOOPS AND OVER HURDLES.

exercise

Although exercise is vital for every dog, whatever its age, size, or breed, each dog has, of course, different requirements. It is not enough just to let your dog run around the garden because dogs that are not adequately exercised may revert to destructive or unacceptable behaviour. Dogs benefit from organized exercise: not only does it provide a physical outlet for their energy, but they love games and find them mentally stimulating. You do not have to stick to a rigorous daily regime that never varies – change the route of your walk, alter the length, or finish off with games in a park on some days, but if you don't want to do this every day, don't. Never forget who is supposed to be in charge!

Generally, bigger breeds need more exercise than smaller ones, but there are exceptions: Saint Bernards, for example, do not enjoy the same sort of terrain and distance that Border collies thrive on. Be aware that once it has been let off the lead, an active young dog will probably run two or three times the distance that you will walk. As a rough guide, a medium-sized dog, such as a golden retriever, will enjoy a walk of about 3 to 4 miles (5 to 6 kilometres) every day, and this distance is the minimum for larger dogs like mature Afghan hounds. Older dogs may prefer two short walks a day rather than one long one.

games

Playing games with your dog emphasizes your control and dominance, but games are also fun and provide mental and physical stimulation. They are a great way of channelling your dog's energies, sustaining its attention, and thus alleviating any risk of destructive behaviour. Make sure that you tailor the games to suit your pet. Don't overstretch old or frail dogs because they will simply become frustrated, while strenuous activity may endanger their health.

You can generally rely on the tried-and-tested game of fetch, in which you throw a stick for your dog to chase and retrieve, but there are a variety of doggy toys available, too. Use Frisbees, balls, and tug toys to amuse your dog. It will enjoy trying to catch a Frisbee and then returning it to you. Dogs love ball games and will relish simply chasing a ball because this reflects natural canine behaviour in chasing prey. Try playing catch and drop by throwing a ball for your dog to catch and then encouraging it to surrender the ball to you. (Never throw a ball directly at a dog in case it injures it – throw it away from the dog so that it can jump for the ball.) If your dog enjoys playing tug-of-war, make sure that the tug toy is robust enough to stand the strain. Indoor games, like hunt the treat or hide and seek, are also stimulating and fun.

It is important to finish a session of games with a human "victory," otherwise the dog will think that it is the dominant partner. When you have finished playing, put the toys away in a bag or box that is inaccessible to the dog. This will teach it that they are your toys and that it can only play with them when you allow it. These toys should be distinct from the

TWO DOGS ENJOY A GAME OF "TUG."

one or two items that are your dog's toys, however, which should be available to it all of the time.

PLAYING WITH OTHER DOGS

Dogs enjoy playing with each other, although females are usually more willing to play than males, who may appear territorial at first. Dogs are likely to meet others when out for a walk in an area that they regard as neutral territory. Let the dogs sniff each other, but watch their body language for any signs of aggression, such as staring eye contact. If this happens, divert their attention with a toy. Fighting is less likely between dogs of different sexes, but it is sensible to keep the dogs on their leads during their first meeting. If appropriate, praise your dog for its calm and alert behaviour.

INTRODUCE OLDER DOGS TO PUPPIES. DO NOT LEAVE THEM ALONE UNTIL THEY ARE USED TO EACH OTHER.

training

Training falls into several different categories. Firstly, behavioural training teaches a dog basic "good manners," including how to behave around people, how to walk on a lead, and house-training. Secondly, obedience training teaches a dog to perform specific activities like walking to heel or sitting and staying. Thirdly, activity training trains a dog in actions, such as retrieving, herding, or agility performances.

Training helps to establish the human position as pack leader. If a dog respects its owner, it will want to obey him or her, so when training your dog, do not shout or become angry if it does not obey you, but instead persevere and take the time to teach your dog commands. Remember that its "disobedience" may simply be caused by puzzlement and a break-down in communication: if it doesn't understand what you want, it can't carry out your commands. Being shouted at or physically punished will both scare a dog, causing it to become apprehensive around an owner who displays this kind of behaviour (and which may actually teach the dog itself to become aggressive). The most effective

IF TWO DOGS MEET, THEY WILL INVARIABLY SNIFF EACH OTHER TO LEARN ABOUT SEX, LOCALITY, AND DOMINANCE.

punishment for a disobedient dog is to ignore it. Because most dogs want attention and to feel that they are part of the pack, withdrawing your attention (including not looking at it) for ten minutes will probably have a greater effect than administering any physical or verbal punishment.

A daily routine of twenty minutes or more will help to reinforce obedience training. Overnight success is unlikely, however, so be patient and consistent. Praise your dog frequently and extravagantly to encourage it. It helps to make the command word part of a praise phrase, for example, by saying "Lovely sit" in an pleased tone of voice. Including the command word within a praise phrase thus serves to reinforce the action without actually repeating the command itself.

It is relatively straightforward to teach young dogs most commands, and training itself is much easier if you begin with a young puppy. We have all heard the

HAND SIGNALS (LIKE THIS FOR "STOP") ARE USED TO REINFORCE VERBAL COMMANDS WHILE TRAINING.

phrase "You can't teach an old dog new tricks," so bear this in mind and work patiently with your pet.

introducing children and dogs

Children must be taught how to treat a dog properly, but, equally, dogs must learn how to behave around children. Dogs recognize that children, who are smaller than adults (and often smaller than a dog), are not "pack leaders," so may try to dominate them by nipping or growling.

Make sure that your children do not tease dogs by pulling their tails, invading their personal space, trying to use them for rides, or squeezing them as though they were teddies. Children should also learn that not every dog is friendly and that they should approach all dogs with caution. Explain to them why some dogs may jump up at them and how to react – it is important that small children realize that if they throw up their hands in horror and squeal, the dog may think they are playing and continue jumping up. Never leave a child and a dog alone together until a child is both old enough to understand these rules and physically large enough to dominate the dog.

CHILDREN MUST LEARN TO TREAT DOGS PROPERLY.

HOW TO INTRODUCE A CHILD TO YOUR DOG

1 Put a lead on your dog. Let the child approach it, but make sure that he or she maintains eye contact with you rather than the dog. A dog will feel threatened by a staring child because it interprets staring as aggressive behaviour.

2 Let the child stroke the dog along its side, but tell the child not to pat its head.

3 Praise the dog for its good behaviour if appropriate, but reprimand it if it snaps or growls.

Dogs should be taught to lie down and relax while children are playing around them, even if they are doing something exciting like playing with a ball.

Once you are confident that your dog can cope with older children, it will probably be able to deal with toddlers. If your dog is particularly prone to guarding or chasing, however, or if it has ever threatened anyone, it is sensible to muzzle it in the presence of toddlers.

Dogs are generally curious about babies, so if one has recently joined your household, ask a friend or your partner to help you to introduce the dog to your new offspring. Babies' flailing limbs and cries may startle even the most placid of animals, so it's important that your dog becomes used to the new arrival. One of you should hold the baby and the other the dog's lead. Let the dog see and sniff the baby, but not touch it. If the dog behaves well, praise it and play with it while the baby is in the room. It is also sensible to feed the dog in the baby's presence to show it that it has not been supplanted in your affections.

But remember: however gentle your pet, never, ever leave it alone with a baby or small child.

WITH CARE, DOGS AND CHILDREN MAKE GREAT FRIENDS.

ADMINISTER REWARDS FOR GOOD BEHAVIOUR.

encouraging good behaviour

The best way of encouraging a dog to do what you want is to use positive reinforcement, that is, to reward good behaviour and ignore, or gently correct, bad behaviour. Physical or verbal punishment is not only unacceptable, but self-defeating. A reward should increase the occurrence of the desired behaviour; a correction should decrease it.

It is important to be consistent in your behaviour and to remain patient – it is all too easy for a dog to confuse rewards and corrections. For example, if your dog is on the other side of a field and persistently ignores your calls, you may become cross. If you shout at it or otherwise show your anger when it finally returns, you will actually be punishing the dog for obeying your command (however slowly!) when you should have rewarded it. A dog associates corrections or rewards with its most recent action, so in this case it will associate returning to its owner with being punished.

USE OF FOOD?

The use of food as a motivation for learning is the subject of controversy. Most trainers seem to agree that it certainly helps in the initial stages of teaching a dog a new command, but others believe that dogs should obey their owners simply because they have been told to do so. Some people simply dislike using food as a reward.

Dogs undeniably perform better when there is the prospect of a reward in sight, whether it is a snack, a squeaky toy, or just verbal praise. The trick is discovering what makes your dog work most productively.

When teaching a new command, reward the dog with a treat the first few times that it performs well, then reward it randomly. This way, the dog will try even harder to earn the reward.

DOGS USUALLY PERFORM BETTER IF FOOD IS OFFERED.

USE A MUZZLE TO CURB AGGRESSIVE DOGS.

SPECIAL EQUIPMENT

It is unlikely that you will need to acquire extra equipment for any of the training exercises included in this book. However, some excitable dogs or particularly large breeds may be easier to control if they are fitted with a head halter or body harness. Dogs with delicate windpipes or those with strong necks and small heads may also be more comfortable wearing a body harness than a lead. Head halters are similar to horse halters in that they pull the dog's head downward if it tries to run off. They are especially useful for controlling large dogs. (See Chapter 2, for more information about harnesses, halters, and leads.)

Consider fitting a muzzle to your dog if it is a persistent scavenger and eater of unsuitable items or if it is destructive or seems aggressive. It may be prudent to muzzle your dog when it meets babies or small children for the first time, too. Dogs adjust very quickly to basket muzzles, which are spacious enough to enable barking and panting. Never leave a muzzle on an unsupervised dog.

A BODY HARNESS MAY SUIT YOUR DOG BEST.

Training Tips

• Train your dog in a quiet area where there are no distractions.

• Never become angry with your dog or administer physical punishment.

• Reward your dog (with food, a toy, or encouraging words) as soon as it has performed a task successfully.

• Keep training sessions short (ten to fifteen minutes to begin with) so that the dog does not become bored.

• Concentrate on encouraging your dog to master one task at a time.

• Try to make training fun!

basic commands

RECALL TRAINING: "COME!"

"Come!" is a vital command, without which no progress can be made with further training. Begin recall training inside before moving on to an enclosed area outside. Don't let your dog off the lead if there is any danger of it running off and not returning. Never call your dog over to reprimand it because it will associate the action with punishment and will therefore be reluctant to repeat the experience.

INSIDE

1 Stand a short distance away from your dog, holding a food treat in your hand. Let the dog see the treat and then say its name, followed by the command "Come!"

2 As the dog comes to you, praise it in a warm voice by saying "Good dog." Bend your knees to bring the treat closer to the dog and open your arms in a welcoming manner.

3 Once the dog has reached you, kneel down so that you are level with it, praise it, give it the treat, and stroke it.

OUTSIDE (IN AN ENCLOSED SPACE)

1 Many dogs, and particularly puppies, dislike being kept in control and will run off once they've been let off the lead. If this happens, it won't want to surrender its freedom either, so let it run around for a few minutes. When it slows down, call it by name, and then say "Come!"

2 Your dog will probably respond by taking a step or two towards you. Praise it for this, saying "Good dog."

3 Take one step backwards and encourage your dog to come closer by patting your leg to show where you want it to go. If it comes, do not instantly put its lead on, but pat it on the head, give it a treat, tell it how good it is ... and then attach the lead.

4 It will probably take time and patience to train your dog to come on command, and it is unlikely to perform first time. If it comes halfway towards you and then wanders off, move out of its line of sight and it should follow you out of curiosity. Never punish your dog for failing to respond. Instead continue practising until it responds immediately. When you are sure that it has mastered the routine, try it out in an open space.

Troubleshooting

If your dog does not respond to edible treats, use a toy to encourage it. If it is easily distracted, use a squeaky toy to get its attention.

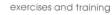

"SIT!"

When your dog has learned to obey the command "Come!," it's time to teach it to sit on command. It is possible to teach some dogs to do this simply by saying "Sit!" and gently pushing down their rump. Others may require more formal training, however.

Troubleshooting

If the dog refuses to sit, hold its collar in one hand and press its hindquarters down with the other while saying "Sit!" Once it has accomplished this, show it that you are pleased with it by praising it.

1 Put a lead on the dog and talk quietly it, keeping the atmosphere calm. Face the dog and then move away, holding the lead in your left hand and a snack treat in your right.

2 Tell the dog to come to you and, when it arrives, gradually move your right hand up and over its head. The dog will watch the treat and, as you see it bend its legs to sit down, give the command "Sit!" If it does, praise the dog and give it the snack.

3 Practise this command on your dog and gradually reduce the food rewards until a verbal command alone does the trick.

"STAY!"

Teach your dog to stay once it has learned to "Sit!"

1 Attach a lead to the dog's collar. Command the dog to sit, and then, holding the lead loosely, step away from it. Now give the command "Stay!" You can reinforce the command with a hand signal, by holding the palm of your hand in front of its face. (Remember that you must be consistent, so if you decide to use the hand signal, you must do so every time.)

PUPPIES MUST LEARN TO SIT STILL WHILE A LEAD IS PUT ON.

2 Walk slowly around the dog in a circle, maintaining eye contact with it. If it tries to get up, make it sit down again. If it stays still for the count of five, go back to it, praise it, and give it a treat. Repeat the exercise, gradually moving farther away for longer periods.

3 Once your dog has mastered it, repeat the whole exercise, but this time drop the lead. While your dog is sitting obediently, give it a treat and praise it. Make sure that you do this before allowing it to move.

DO NOT LET YOUR DOG OFF THE LEAD IN A PUBLIC PLACE UNTIL YOU ARE SURE THAT IT WILL RESPOND TO YOUR COMMANDS.

Troubleshooting

This exercise may be quite difficult for your dog because its natural instinct is to go to you. If it tries to get up and does not stay, hold its collar with one hand while pressing down its hindquarters with the other.

"DOWN!"

As your dog gets older, train it to lie down while distracting activity is going on around it. If you can teach your dog to obey this command in such circumstances, you will be able to exert control over it if it tries to jump up at people. Initial training should take place in a quiet place, however.

1 Conceal a treat in one hand. Tell your dog to sit and then let it see the treat in your hand.

2 Move the treat-holding hand to the floor while saying "Down!" The dog will probably move into the "down" position in order to reach the treat. Reward and praise your dog – and keep practising.

Troubleshooting

If a puppy is reluctant to lie down, raise it into the begging position and then, with one palm under each of its forelegs, lie it down and praise it. If it tries to jump up, hold it down by gently pushing on its withers for a few seconds.

"DOWN AND STAY!"

1 With your dog on a lead in the "down" position, give the command "Stay!" and walk away, still holding the leash. Maintain eye contact with your dog as you are walking away. Repeat the command "Stay!" and praise your dog. When practicing this exercise, gradually make it stay down for longer periods.

2 Train your dog to stay down when you are out of sight by repeating steps 1 to 3 and then leaving the room. Peer through a crack or use a mirror to make sure that it does not move. After a few minutes, return and praise your dog while it is still lying down. Do this calmly so that you don't excite it.

Troubleshooting

If the dog gets up while you are out of the room, return, make it lie down again, repeat the "Stay!" command and then remain in the room, moving around as it watches you.

WALKING AT HEEL WITHOUT A LEAD: "HEEL!"

Because they enjoy human company, puppies especially naturally follow their owners. This makes it reasonably simple to train a dog to walk by your side without a lead from a very young age.

1 Position the dog on your left. Hold a treat in your right hand and gently grasp its collar with your left. Call the dog by name and let it see the treat.

2 Walk in a straight line and let the dog follow the treat as you give the command "Heel!"

3 Say "Wait!" and then bend down next to the dog's right side to show it the treat.

4 Holding the snack near the dog's nose, make a right turn and repeat the command "Heel!" The dog will speed up to follow you and the treat.

5 Holding its collar with your left hand, gently steer the dog to the left. Position your right, snack-holding, hand at a low level so that the dog follows you round to the left.

6 Give the dog its reward and lots of praise.

WALKING AT HEEL ON A LEAD: "HEEL!"

Most dogs learn to walk at heel on a lead as puppies. Dogs should never be allowed to pull on their leads, which results in cross owners with sore shoulder muscles and dogs that are gasping for breath – no way to take an invigorating walk.

It is best to begin training your dog to walk at heel somewhere quiet, such as your garden. The aim of the exercise is for your dog to follow you closely, walking at your pace, with its head close to your left leg. Hold the lead in your right hand, taking up the slack with your left hand. (This is the most natural stance for right-handed individuals, but can, of course, be reversed if you are left-handed.)

5 To turn right, gently push your dog with your left hand and repeat the command "Heel!" To make a left turn, use a food treat to entice your dog to move forward and follow you, again saying "Heel!"

TROUBLESHOOTING

Climbing up the lead: respond by saying "No!" or "Off!" very sternly. Tell the dog to sit and then start the exercise again. Try training the dog in a quiet spot inside, where it will not become excited or distracted.

Immobile dog: if the dog refuses to shift and collapses onto the floor, try encouraging it with a favourite toy. Do not shout or become angry. Cajole it into obeying by using lots of praise so that its confidence increases.

Pulling forward: tell the dog to sit every time that it pulls forward. If your dog is very lively, try using a head halter.

1 Begin by attaching a lead to the dog's collar. Call the dog by name and then say "Heel!" in a commanding voice. If it follows you, walk forward with the lead held slackly.

2 If it fails to respond, jerk the lead firmly and repeat the command. If it tries to walk ahead of you, slide your left hand down the lead to its collar and gently pull it back.

3 After a couple of minutes of walking at heel, praise your dog fulsomely.

4 If it slows down or tries to wander off, pull sharply on the lead and say "Heel!" It will quickly learn that it is more comfortable to follow you as required.

RETRIEVING

Retrieving is quite an advanced skill, but most breeds respond excellently to training. Use something like an old dog toy rather than a stick or a ball, as the dog will find it easier to identify. First, show the dog the object you wish him to retrieve. Let him sniff it and perhaps clutch it in his mouth. Do not let him play with it, however.

2 Throw the object across the garden or field and give the command "Fetch!" Your dog will probably not need any more encouragement to chase across the field and collect the object.

3 Once the dog has the object, say "Come" to make him approach you, then tell him to "Give" to surrender the object. Reward him with lots of praise and patting. As a final reward, you can return the object to the dog.

correcting inappropriate behaviour

Dogs that have been well trained from an early age are unlikely to provide major problems as they get older. However, poorly trained animals may exhibit some bad habits that are both annoying and dangerous. If you adopted your dog from a rescue home, you may have to work quite hard to correct a few anti-social facets of its behaviour. Although some problems are the result of poor training, others are simply uncontrolled natural canine behaviour, while still others result from boredom, anxiety, or frustration. This section, as well as Chapter 1, may help to explain why your dog behaves as it does.

TRAINING CAN HELP CORRECT BAD BEHAVIOUR.

BARKING PROBLEMS

It is natural for dogs to bark when they are excited, frustrated, bored, or want to convey a warning when they are in "guard" mode, so the arrival of visitors will often precipitate a lot of noise. A barking dog is a useful deterrent against intruders, and short bursts of barking are a natural outlet for canine excitement, but sometimes dogs bark simply to gain attention, sometimes out of fear, and sometimes as a sign of anxiety when they have been left alone.

BARKING CAN IRRITATE, SO SHOULD BE ADDRESSED.

Prolonged episodes of barking can irritate neighbours, not to mention dog-owners, and in some cases are a sign that your dog is unhappy, so it is a problem that must be addressed. The following exercise should help to control the problem.

An Exercise to Control Barking: "Quiet!"

Because repetition is the key to making it work, this exercise requires patience.

1 Show your dog a toy, but don't let it play with it. Reward it when it barks.

2 Put the toy in your pocket and verbally praise your dog when it barks, occasionally handing out a more tempting treat.

3 Watch the dog closely, give the command "Speak!" and reward the dog when it barks.

4 When the dog understands the "Speak!" command, say "Quiet!" and reward the dog with the toy when it is silent. Put the toy away if it begins to bark again.

5 Repeat the exercise, but this time move further away from your dog.

DOGS NEED TRAINING TO AVOID BECOMING ANXIOUS OR STRESSED.

Do not shout at your dog because it will think that you are simply sharing its excitement. It is best to ignore its barking for as long as you can and instead to accustom the dog to the events that wind it up. Initiate some obedience training to impose limits on the dog's behaviour on the occasions when it would normally bark. So if, for example, your dog scares the postman by barking ferociously every time that he approaches the house, train your dog to sit quietly during his daily visit. You could also incorporate a command that allows it to bark when you want it to, such as when visitors arrive. Use the training techniques illustrated earlier in this chapter, and remember that because altering this type of behaviour is unlikely to succeed overnight, you'll need to persevere. With time and patience, however, it is possible to train a dog to bark on command or under specific conditions.

Dogs that bark as a result of guarding behaviour usually stop as soon as the "threat" to their territory has disappeared (unlike excited dogs, which continue to bark). Some dogs "guard" the house because they are unsure about who controls the arrival of visitors. In such cases, it is important to teach your dog that you are in charge (although its guarding behaviour will probably continue when you are away and it has been left at home). Owners of dominant dogs like this must exert their control as "pack leader" by imposing firm obedience training on their pets. Teach your dog to earn your attention by obeying a command, for example, but ignore it if it tries to demand it.

Attention-seeking dogs bark to attract notice and then stop as soon as someone approaches them (this behaviour is often learned as a puppy). It can be exceptionally annoying if your dog barks while you are on the phone or talking to someone, behaviour that is simply the result of your dog feeling left out. Cure this problem by ignoring your dog's methods of attention-seeking, such as barking, nudging your hand, or dropping toys expectantly at your feet. Tell it to sit and ask before you stroke it and give it all of your attention – it will need periods when it has your undivided attention, so play games and carry out training exercises for at least an hour a day.

Dogs that bark due to separation anxiety are often very attached to their owners and find being alone highly stressful. If this is the case, make sure that your dog has been well exercised before leaving it and train it to become used to spending time alone. Teach it to obey the "Quiet!" command and then leave it in a room for a couple of minutes. If the dog begins barking, make a loud noise to startle it and then return to the room and praise it when it is quiet before leaving again. You will probably have to repeat this exercise several times, but once your dog has become accustomed to the idea of being quiet, build up the length of time that it is left alone. It also helps to give it a toy with your scent on it.

AGGRESSION

MUZZLE AN AGGRESSIVE OR DANGEROUS DOG.

Aggression is one of the most common problems that dog behaviourists are asked to deal with. Dogs behave aggressively for a variety of reasons, and while some will direct their aggression only towards other animals, others will behave aggressively toward shumans.

DOGS CAN BE TRAINED BY A HUMAN "PACK LEADER".

DOMINANT DOGS MAY TRY TO IMPOSE THEIR WILL ON MORE SUBMISSIVE ANIMALS.

If a dog considers itself to be the dominant animal in the "pack," it may try to exert its power by threatening family members, especially vulnerable ones, such as children. Even small dogs like West Highland terriers will aim a nip at an adult owner if they have not been trained to accept their status. Animals who regard themselves as top dog may also damage their owner's possessions. A dominant dog will often stare directly at strangers, try to go through doors first, and expect an immediate response to their demands for attention. Do not confuse the behaviour of a dominant dog with that of a frightened one — although both animals will snarl, and possibly bite, the frightened dog will probably cower behind its owner and will be apprehensive when encountering new faces and situations.

Dominant aggression is treated by training the dog to accept its position as a subordinate member of the "pack." It is important to minimize the risk that your dog poses to others, so fit a muzzle or adjustable head halter before taking it for walks; this will also encourage obedience. Groom your dog at least once a day because this reinforces human dominance. Fit a house line so that you can control its movements more easily. Do not allow it to jump on to furniture and ignore all of its requests for attention. Do not respond until it stops making demands, and then command it to sit before stroking it. Ensure that you eat before the dog does because in wild wolf packs the leader always eats first: prepare the dog's food, but eat your meal first, only feeding the dog when you have finished. When exercising your dog, also initiate some retrieving exercises, which will further emphasize who is in control. Do not give it any treats while you are carrying out this training.

TWO DOGS TRY TO WARN OFF A HORSE AND RIDER.

STARING AND LEANING FORWARD ARE DANGER SIGNS.

EXCITABLE DOGS JUMP UP TO GREET PEOPLE.

Dogs behave aggressively towards other dogs either to defend their own territory or because they have been poorly socialized and are unused to the company of other animals. Male dogs are more likely to exhibit this type of behaviour than females, and neutering reduces the problem in young dogs (around two years of age). Actual fighting is preceded by the display of aggressive body language: the dog will stare intently at its adversary and will assume a forward stance, with its ears and tail raised. It may also snarl and bare its teeth (and if your dog becomes involved in a fight with another dog, be wary of intervening in case you are bitten).

Prevention is possible, although you must first learn to recognize the signs of brewing aggression. If you notice your dog making threatening eye contact with another animal, for example, divert its attention, if necessary physically turning its head away. Think ahead and take a toy with you, and if its aggression seems to be escalating, command it to sit and use the toy to reward good behavior, thus diverting its attention. When a dog pulls on a leash, its feelings of aggression increase, so do not exacerbate the situation by forcibly pulling it back. Anticipate the problem by muzzling your dog if necessary.

In order to decrease the likelihood of a dog fight, reinforce your dog's recall training (see page 122), first at home and then in an open area within sight of another dog. Reward your dog when it ignores the other animal, or at least when it does not demonstrate hostile behaviour.

ANXIETY

After aggression, separation anxiety is probably the second most common behavioral problem in dogs and is characterized by a dog that whines when left alone and is extremely excited and clingy when its owner returns. The dog may follow its owner from room to room, demonstrating great affection, trying to maintain eye contact, and demanding as much physical contact as possible. When left alone, it may howl, bark, or wreck the room that it is in as it tries to find a way out. Such dogs must be trained to lessen their overattachment to their owners and to feel more secure when left alone.

Try to discourage your dog from following you around by shutting doors and asking other family members and friends to entertain it. In this way, it will gradually become less dependent on you.

Gradually increase the length of time that the dog is left alone. It may help to leave a radio on and to place one item of your clothing on its bed and another on the other side of the closed door.

Ignore your dog for about twenty minutes before your departure and for twenty minutes after your return. Do not greet it until it has calmed down.

JUMPING UP

Excited dogs often jump up to greet their owners, when they know that it is time for a walk, or if they hear a visitor arriving. Some breeds are more likely to jump up to solicit attention than others: big, assertive breeds may try to enforce their dominant position in such a way, while others, such as standard poodles, do it to beg for affection. All puppies greet their mother by licking her face, and young dogs aged

TEACH A JUMPING DOG TO CALM DOWN.

between six and eighteen months are likely to reproduce this behaviour with their owners. Some

owners encourage their dogs to jump up by slapping their thighs, but many people, especially children, find this type of excited behaviour unsettling. It is generally better to teach your dog to greet you with all four paws on the ground.

If your dog jumps up at you, turn away, withdraw eye contact, and say "No!" or "Down!" sternly. Tell the dog to sit and then greet it, praising it for obeying you.

CHASING

Dogs that persistently chase vehicles are both annoying and dangerous in that they are endangering both themselves and others, especially drivers, who may be distracted by them. It is very difficult to overcome this problem because all dogs are natural chasers: they chase in order to scare off predators, and because cars and cyclists (the usual targets) rarely stop, the dog will be satisfied that it has succeeded. One instantaneous preventative measure is to ask a friend, armed with a water pistol, to cycle past the offending dog. As the dog chases the bike, the cyclist should stop and squirt the dog, at the same time saying "No!" firmly.

Generations of selective breeding have failed to eliminate the dog's basic instinct to chase prey, and this problem is most likely to surface on, or near, farms. Dogs must be kept on a lead if they are anywhere near farm animals; farmers are within their rights to shoot dogs that are known to worry sheep and cattle. If your dog seems tempted to give chase, divert its attention by throwing a toy in the opposite direction to the other animal and encourage it to chase and retrieve the toy. With luck, the dog will become so absorbed by the game that it will forget its desire to chase the other animal.

DOGS THAT CHASE AUTOMOBILES ARE ANNOYING AND A DANGER TO THEMSELVES RATHER THAN OTHERS.

USE A STAIR GATE TO RESTRICT YOUR DOG'S ACCESS.

DO NOT LET A DOG HOG YOUR FAVOURITE CHAIR.

DESTRUCTIVE BEHAVIOUR

Destructive behaviour is often an outlet for boredom or frustration. Chewing, scratching, destroying soft furnishings or personal possessions – all of these behavioral problems are undesirable, but it is vital to understand what has prompted them in the first place. Puppies chew as part of the teething process, but can be easily trained to turn their attention from shoes and slippers to toys. Older dogs must also be taught what is unacceptable behaviour, although you should also make sure that you remove all tempting articles from sight.

Destructive behaviour, such as wrecking soft furnishings, or even destroying its owner's personal possessions, can become an outlet for an intelligent dog that is lacking in stimulation. Boredom is a major cause of destructive behaviour, and the only solution is to ensure that your dog is mentally stimulated and well exercised. Part of the cure obviously lies in denying the dog access to tempting articles. More importantly, however, if your dog is left alone for long periods, make sure that it has a couple of toys to play with and that it has also enjoyed a long walk, preferably with some obedience training beforehand.

SENSIBLE TRAINING HELPS A DOG UNDERSTAND ACCEPTABLE BEHAVIOUR.

Frustrated dogs may also create damage around the house, often focused in one area. If a dog wants to get outside to chase a cat, for example, it may scratch or chew around a door or window. Owners either need to discover what is upsetting their pet and remedy it if possible or else keep it in a different room, away from the source of frustration. Once again, make sure that the dog is well exercised before leaving it alone and ensure that it has some stimulating toys to play with while you're away, too.

TEACH YOUR DOG TO STAY WHEN YOU LEAVE HOME.

MOUNTING EMBARRASSMENT

Dogs that try to mount table legs or the legs of visitors may initially appear funny, but some people find this type of behaviour embarrassing, and it certainly becomes annoying. Because most male dogs rarely meet females in heat, they often attempt to mount their owners' legs. The simple answer is to neuter a male dog, which will certainly reduce the problem (females also mount things, but spaying has little effect). Like many potential problems, this one is best caught early, so do not allow your puppy or adolescent dog to mount legs – either yours or those of furniture – in order to prevent it becoming a habit that is hard to break in adulthood.

Cold showers and plenty of fresh air sound like old-fashioned remedies, but canine variations on this theme may reduce the problem. Use a water pistol to spray water at a dog that is thrusting into a rug or cushion – the dog will certainly be diverted and probably put off. A dog that mounts anything clearly needs some sort of stimulation, so make sure that it is well exercised. Control the behaviour of an oversexed dog by making it wear a lead or house line. If it tries to mount anything, say "No!" firmly and remove it to another room for a minute. Once it has returned from isolation, ignore it for a few minutes, then tell it to sit, reward it, and play with it.

obedience classes

Obedience classes are not just for badly behaved dogs, or those whose owners want them to pursue a course to shows and trials, and they are especially useful when you are new to dog-owning. Held all over the country, vets, libraries, and breed associations should be able to recommend some obedience classes near you.

Classes are offered for almost every age of dog. Puppy socialization classes, intended for dogs (accompanied by their owners) under sixteen weeks of age, are an excellent way of introducing your puppy to other dogs and people. They also provide a good basis for further training. You can learn about basic training from professional dog-trainers at classes that are open to owners of puppies, as well as older dogs. Owners who want to encourage their dogs to fulfill their potential in agility, tracking, retrieving, and other specialist dog sports should be able to find advanced training classes to suit their specifications.

Whatever type of class you and your dog attend, make sure that you are happy with the trainer's techniques and the number of dogs in the class. If your dog is a persistent offender in one way or another, it may benefit from weekly sessions with a personal trainer.

CLASSES HELP NEW OWNERS TRAIN THEIR DOGS.

DOGS BENEFIT FROM EXPERT TUITION, AS DO OWNERS.

LEARNING TO STAY.

FIND A CLASS WITH A LOW TEACHER–PUPIL RATIO.

exercises and training   145

SIX

a dog's life

diet

Dogs are carnivores. Their digestive system is designed to absorb protein from meat and their teeth are configured for ripping flesh. Having said that, however, dogs, like humans, are not equipped to survive on an all-meat diet. Like us, dogs need a judicious mix of nutrients that contains the right balance of carbohydrates, fats, proteins, minerals, and vitamins. Dogs are descended from scavenging ancestors and can survive on an intermittent diet of virtually anything, but this would undoubtedly result in nutritional deficiencies.

Most adult dogs should have one or two meals a day and continuous access to a bowl of water. Many dogs have a main meal in the morning and a few dog biscuits in the evening. Dogs' energy levels vary throughout their life, and their calorie requirements reflect this. Puppies have a higher calorie requirement than adult dogs, working dogs need more food than sedentary animals, and older dogs will probably eat less than when they were younger. Always seek professional advice if you are unsure about how much to feed your pet.

DOGS NEED REGULAR AND HEALTHY MEALS.

DRIED FOOD ALLOWS OWNERS TO FEED THEIR DOGS A PRECISE CALORIFIC AMOUNT.

The essential nutrients for a dog are broadly similar to those required by humans. Protein is necessary for growth and plays a vital role in building cell membranes and regenerating healing tissues within the body. It is derived from either plant or animal sources, but plant proteins lack some of the amino acids necessary for mammalian health. Carbohydrates provide much of the body's energy and, for dogs, are derived from biscuit meal, rice bread, or commercially made dog biscuits and snacks. Finally, fats are essential as a concentrated energy source and to provide fatty acids or polyunsaturates. Minerals, such as calcium, phosphorus, and salt, and vitamins are usually present in a well-balanced diet, but can be provided as supplements if a vet deems it necessary.

CALCULATE YOUR DOG'S WEIGHT.

WEIGHT-WATCHING

It is important not to overfeed your dog, because obesity will make it unhealthy, placing extra strain on its joints, digestive system, and internal organs. Ultimately, a fat dog will have a shorter life expectancy than a thinner one, and most obese dogs are overweight because they are being overfed and underexercised. A healthy dog should exhibit some sort of waist when viewed from above, and you should be able to feel, but not see, its ribs. Do not become obsessed by your dog's weight, however, and never impose a crash diet on your pampered pooch. Ask your vet for advice if you think that your dog is overweight and needs to lose a few pounds.

Regularly weighing your dog will enable you to spot any tendency towards obesity, as well as weight loss, which may be a sign of illness. The easiest method of weighing your dog is to hold it while standing on the bathroom scales and then to subtract your weight from the figure shown. If you have a large dog, try to coax it to stand on the scales alone. Pedigree breeders and vets will be able to give you an idea of the average weight for your dog's breed or size.

WHICH FOOD?

Modern dogs – or rather their owners – are faced with an almost bewildering choice of food, ranging

PIGS' EARS ARE A CANINE DELICACY.

from the traditional table scraps to scientifically adjusted diets that target animals with special requirements, such as puppies or nursing bitches. Deciding which food is right for your dog is not easy. It is important to bear in mind the breed and size of the animal, and how much time you can devote to preparing your dog's meals. Some owners prefer to prepare fresh food for their pets, but not only is this time-consuming, surveys have shown that over 90 percent of home-made dog foods are nutritionally unbalanced. Pet-food manufacturers have spent vast sums of money researching the field of dog food in order to create products that combine convenience, the best nutritional mix, and palatability. It is not only easier to use manufactured pet food than to prepare fresh food yourself, but ensures that your dog receives the correct mix of vitamins and nutrients. Make sure that you follow the manufacturer's recommendations for portion size (see also the table on page 155).

There are three main types of commercially available dog food – moist or wet foods, complete dry meals, and semi-moist food – along with special foods and treats.

MOIST OR WET FOODS

Most of the tinned dog foods that are sold in supermarkets are carefully calibrated to provide dogs with a healthy diet. Some provide a complete diet, while others have a lower carbohydrate level and must be supplemented with dog meal. They are composed of meat, offal, poultry, or fish and incorporate vitamin and mineral supplements. As a caveat, they often have a high protein content, which can make some dogs very energetic and overexcited, which may be a problem in a big, dominant dog.

COMPLETE DRY MEALS

These products are extremely convenient. A mixture of cereals and protein, they are available in the form of pellets or other shapes and are coated with fat to improve their palatability. Some types must be rehydrated with water before consumption. They have as much as four times the calorie content of tinned food and must therefore be fed in smaller portions.

DOGGY TREATS ARE USEFUL AS REWARDS.

DOG BISCUITS MAKE A USEFUL NIGHT-TIME SNACK.

SEMI-MOIST FOOD

Semi-moist food is not intended as the only source of nourishment and must be supplemented with biscuits or meal to provide adequate carbohydrates.

SPECIAL FOODS AND TREATS

Manufacturers also produce special foods, such as high-energy food for puppies and vitamin- and mineral-enriched varieties for elderly dogs or nursing bitches. Some manufacturers provide prescription diets for dogs with specific health problems, such as diabetes, heart trouble, or kidney disorders. These should only be given to a dog on the advice of a vet.

CHEWING A HARD ITEM HELPS CLEAN DOGS' TEETH.

There is also an infinite variety of snacks and treats, from meaty treats and bone-shaped dog biscuits to doggy chocs. Never give your dog human sweets, however, especially chocolate, which can poison dogs if eaten in large enough quantities. So if you offer your dog treats, make sure that they are special doggy snacks and, because they are high in calories, remember to include them in the daily calorie count.

ALTERING A DIET

If you decide to change your dog's food, do so gradually. If you are switching from a wet food to a dry diet, for instance, begin by placing a half-and-half mix in your dog's feeding bowl and gradually reduce the amount of wet food over time – say a week or two.

DENTAL HYGIENE

As a follow-up to feeding your dog well, make sure that you clean its teeth every day. Severe gum and plaque disease can lead to heart problems in older dogs and, at the very least, keeping its teeth and gums clean will prevent unpleasant "dog's breath." Your vet will be able to recommend a canine toothpaste (dogs dislike the minty human varieties) to use to keep your pet's teeth and gums healthy, or else use dilute salt water. Use an adult-sized toothbrush for a large dog

AVOID BONES AND GIVE YOUR DOG A RAWHIDE TOY TO CHEW.

HOW TO CLEAN A DOG'S TEETH

and a small one for a medium-sized or small dog. Special canine toothbrushes are also available.

In some cases, chewing a large, raw (not cooked) bone will help to clean a dog's teeth and massage its gums, but it must be a large bone, such as an ox shank. Never give your dog chicken, fish, or lamb bones or ones that are likely to splinter or become stuck in its throat. Small dogs that are unable to cope with big bones can chew on raw carrots, and an even better option is a chew toy or a rawhide stick, available from pet shops.

1 Settle your dog quietly on the floor or on your lap.

2 Place your left hand across its muzzle, with a finger or thumb under the chin to keep its mouth closed. Using your right hand, gently insert the toothbrush inside its lips.

3 Starting at the back and working forwards, brush the outer surface of the teeth (the tongue does a reasonable job of keeping the inside clean). Move the brush gently in a circular motion – do not scrub the teeth. Make sure that you clean the gum line, too.

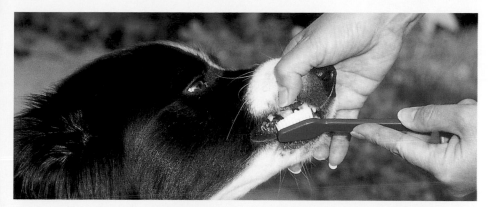

HOLD THE DOG'S JAW WHILE CLEANING ITS TEETH.

IT IS EXTREMELY IMPORTANT TO KEEP A DOG'S TEETH AND GUMS CLEAN AND HEALTHY. CHECK TEETH REGULARLY FOR ANY PROBLEMS. IF IN DOUBT, CONSULT A VET.

DOGGY TOOTHBRUSHES HAVE ANGLED HEADS.

FEEDING GUIDE FOR ADULT DOGS

This chart is simply a rough guide. Individual dogs' food requirements vary according to their activity levels and mood. Remember that this is the daily requirement, not per meal.

Dog size	Approx. daily calorie needs	Tinned food/meal (420 g/14 oz tin)	Semi-moist food	Dry food
Toy breeds less than 4.5 kg (10lb), e.g., Yorkshire terrier, Chihuahua, Pomeranian	210	105 g (4 oz) meat +35 g (1 oz) meal	70 g (2.4 oz)	60 g (2 oz)
Small breeds 4.5-9 kg (10-20 lb), e.g., West Highland terrier, beagle	590	300 g (11 oz) meat +100 g (4 oz) meal	200 g (8 oz)	170 g (6 oz)
Medium breeds 9-22 kg (20-50 lb), e.g., Springer spaniel, Basset hound	900	450 g (16 oz) meat +150 g (5 oz) meal	300 g (11 oz)	260 g (9 oz)
Large breeds 22-34 kg (50-75 lb), e.g., German shepherd, Labrador, Irish setter.	1,680	850 g (30 oz) meat +280 g (10 oz) meal	550 g (19 oz)	480 g (17 oz)
Giant breeds 34-63 kg (74-140 lb), e.g., Great Dane, Newfoundland. Irish wolfhound	2,800	1,400 g (49 oz) meat +460 g (16 oz) meal	900 g (32 oz)	800 g (28 oz)

EATING PROBLEMS

There is no convincing evidence that dogs become bored by being offered the same type of food every day, although some dogs, particularly small breeds, do become fussy about food. In some cases, battles over food are part of the dog's struggle to establish its dominance within its "pack" – in the wild, the pack leader has first choice of food – and it may be trying to assert itself by refusing one food in favour of another.

Do not give in to this behaviour. First check with your vet that your dog is not unhealthy in any way and then impose a new mealtime regime. Leave the food in its bowl for an hour or so and then, if it remains uneaten, remove it. Your dog can survive without food for a couple of days and will give in when it becomes really hungry.

Some dogs appear to like eating grass, and although this is not inherently dangerous, it can lead to infections and disease. It is thought that dogs eat grass to ease stomach discomfort because it often induces vomiting. It may also be a sign that the dog needs more fibre in its diet.

Other dogs seem to delight in eating their own faeces, a condition known as coprophagia. There are various explanations for this habit. It may be that the dog is suffering from a deficiency of certain B vitamins or vitamin K, which is produced by bacteria in the gut. However, the behaviour seems to become habit-forming and is often prevalent among dogs who have been kennelled in unsanitary conditions. Clean up after your dog as quickly as possible to limit the possibility of faeces consumption. In severe cases, your vet can supply a drug called Cythiomate to taint the faeces, which will make the dog feel very ill after it has eaten it.

A HEALTHY DIET PRODUCES A HAPPY AND HEALTHY DOG.

Scavenging is a natural canine habit to which most dogs will succumb if food is left temptingly within reach. Do not let your dog sniff around discarded food when you are out for a walk and keep all foodstuffs out of its reach at home. Persistent scavenging may be a sign of illness: pancreatic insufficiency, for example, increases a dog's appetite, causing it to try to obtain food at every opportunity.

grooming

Regular grooming is important for most dogs, particularly the longer-haired breeds, because it removes dead hair. But grooming is not merely for cosmetic purposes: it is also a valuable means of detecting fleas and other skin parasites, or thorns or burrs that have adhered to the dog's coat during a walk.

Grooming is part of the bonding process between owner and dog, too, and can be very pleasurable and relaxing for the dog. Dogs who are accustomed to being groomed from a young age will settle quickly and enjoy their grooming sessions – as will the owner because it is obviously far easier to groom a compliant dog than a wriggling animal! In addition, it is an important part of your dog's training: by insisting that your pet stands still while you groom it, you are emphasizing your control and dominance.

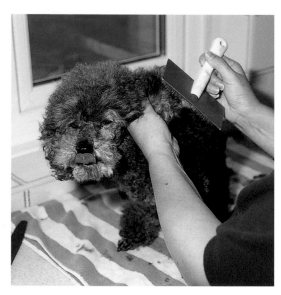

POODLES BENEFIT FROM DAILY GROOMING WITH A SLICKER BRUSH, WHICH UNTANGLES FUR.

Begin by simply grooming a small puppy with a brush and comb – more serious grooming can wait until it is older. Long-coated breeds should be groomed daily in order to prevent their fur from matting; dealing with matted fur is a tricky task which the dog may find painful, so it is worth spending a short time each day grooming your dog to avoid this.

ROUTINE GROOMING

The grooming needs of dogs vary tremendously from breed to breed, but the basics are the same.

Welsh corgis and other short-coated dogs have dense layers of hair close to the skin which both insulates them and is water-resistant. They have another layer of thick, straight hair on top, which needs less attention than that of many other breeds, but their coats do tend to molt, covering their owners and homes in dog hairs. Daily grooming will help to prevent this. Use a stiff brush all over the body (but be sensitive when brushing the head and face) and follow up with a wire-bristled glove. The whole routine will probably take no more than ten minutes.

Smooth-coated dogs require little maintenance, but their coats may provide inadequate protection against the cold and require weekly brushing. Some smooth-coated dogs, such as Great Danes and Dobermans, suffer when the coarse hairs on their body's pressure points (the elbows and hocks) penetrate the skin. Treat these areas with conditioner to soften the hair.

ASK A VET OR PROFESSIONAL GROOMER TO CUT CLAWS IF YOU FIND IT TRICKY.

Rough-coated dogs do not moult in the same way as their short-coated cousins, but they do "cast" every six months or so, when their hair comes out in great chunks, particularly if the dog has not been groomed regularly. Terriers and other rough-coated breeds therefore benefit from a daily brushing-out to prevent the coat from matting. Use a stiff brush and a comb with which to penetrate every knot and make sure that the coat is trimmed regularly, preferably by a professional groomer.

Silky-coated breeds, such as King Charles spaniels and Irish setters, need the same attention as rough-coated breeds, but do not use too stiff a brush. Their coats may become rather heavy and will require trimming once or twice a year.

Long-haired dogs are the most time-consuming to groom, making grooming them a labour of love. A dog with fine, silky hair, such as an Afghan hound or Yorkshire terrier, will need a thorough daily grooming with a slicker brush, pin brush, and wide-toothed comb for the feathering on the back of the legs. Be careful not to brush too hard or pull on any tangles in case you hurt your dog.

Place your dog on a table. (Although grooming can be carried out on the floor, dogs associate this area with play, so it may be difficult to keep it still. Dogs must be trained to sit still for grooming or veterinary treatment at an early age.) Put one hand around the dog's chest and shoulders to steady it and then, using a hound glove or rubber brush, brush down its body (starting at the back of the neck and moving to the sides, then between the hind legs and under the body) to remove dead or loose hairs. Note that dogs are sensitive about their paws, and especially their tails and anal regions, being touched. Talk to your dog, especially when you are grooming its head and face, and reward it at the end of the session.

PROFESSIONAL GROOMING

Some dogs – poodles, Afghan hounds, and Old English sheepdogs, for example – will benefit from the attentions of a professional dog-groomer, in other words, a trip to the proverbial poodle parlour every month or so. This is worthwhile, not only because it will ensure that your dog looks its very best, but you will probably pick up some professional tips and hints to help you to keep your dog in top condition. If you intend to show your dog, professional grooming is a necessity.

Very wiry-coated dogs like schnauzers, border terriers, and Airedales may need professional attention, too. Their coats must be stripped every three to four months, with the dead hair being pulled out by hand or with a stripping knife. This is completely painless and helps to maintain their naturally wiry coats. It can be rather a long job, and may best be tackled in short sessions over two or three days. Alternatively, clip the coat regularly and ask a professional groomer to trim around the face.

Many dogs enjoy the attention lavished on them while being groomed. A professional dog groomer has the skills to tidy up any breed of dog, but long-haired dogs in particular will benefit from his or her skills.

A dog-grooming salon is equipped with a variety of equipment to make washing a dog easier than it may be at home. The dog is restrained with a loose leash clipped to a wall chain.

Once washed, the fluffy ears of this spaniel are gently dried with a hairdryer.

Dog-groomers can offer an expert service with a high level of attention to detail. Their experience means that they are able to wash even the most fractious dog quickly and with the minimum of fuss.

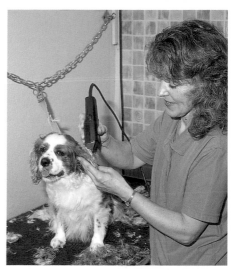

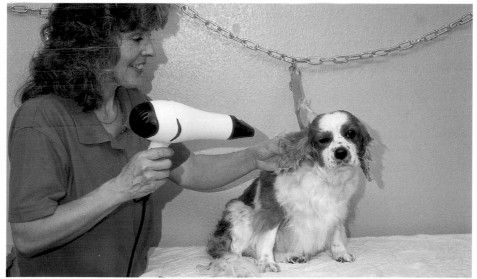

A REGULAR HEALTH CHECK

Grooming also provides an opportunity for you to check your dog's general health. Every few days, clean away the mucus around its eyes, using a different piece of dampened cotton batting for each eye. If your dog has a wrinkled face or many folds of skin, clean around these, too, checking for odour or inflammation.

Lift the flaps of the ears to check for inflammation or redness (if the dog is scratching around an ear, take it to the vet for examination). Dogs with long ears, such as spaniels, must be carefully checked.

Next, check your dog's teeth and gums for inflammation. If it is reluctant to open its mouth, hold its lower jaw firmly with one hand while blocking its nostrils. Use a soft toothbrush to remove debris and

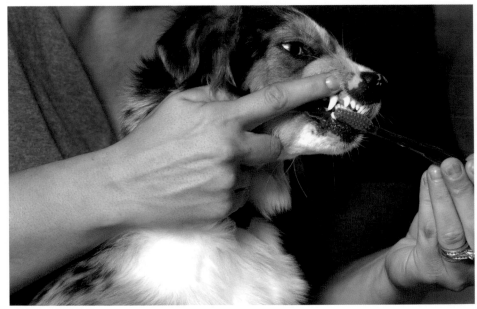

USE A SOFT BRUSH TO CLEAN CANINE TEETH.

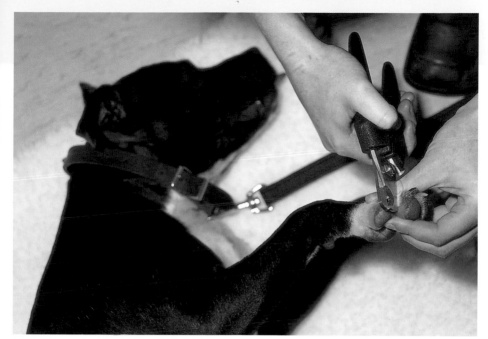

THE CLAWS OF SOME DOGS REQUIRE THE ATTENTIONS OF A VET.

massage the gums every day (see also dental hygiene, pages 154 to 157).

Inspect your dog's anal region and clean away accumulated debris. If your dog is dragging its bottom along the ground, its anal sacs may need emptying (ask your vet for advice about this).

Examine its paws, too, especially between the toes, and remove any matted fur, grit, small stones, or seeds that may have become trapped. Grass seeds are prone to stick and can be removed with tweezers,

although it may be sensible to consult a vet. Check the pads and clean off any mud with a moistened piece of cotton batting. Trim away any long fur to prevent foreign bodies becoming lodged in it.

Regular walks along hard pavements will help to keep your dog's claws short, but, if necessary, cut them using specially angled, doggy nailclippers. Cut above the quick, the pink area on the claw – this is usually obvious in clear nails, but may be more difficult to see in dark ones. If you are unsure, a vet will show you the best way to trim your dog's claws.

1 This dog is small enough to be washed in a basin. Use either baby shampoo or a special dog shampoo.

2 After shampooing, gently rinse off the suds with warm water, avoiding the eye area.

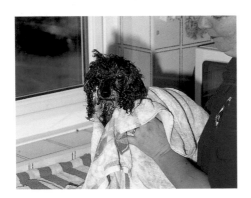

3 Wrap your dog in an old towel and rub him dry before he has a chance to shower you with water.

4 Finally, dry your dog with a hairdryer on a low setting. Keep it moving so that you do not scorch the animal.

WASHING A DOG

Left to their own devices, dogs keep themselves reasonably clean by rolling on the ground, scratching, and chewing at matted fur and licking themselves. Because they also love to roll in mud – and worse – there will undoubtedly be a time when a sign of your dog's presence wafts into the room before it does. Time for a bath!

Unless your dog has become extremely muddy or smelly, it will probably only need a bath once every couple of months (although some breeds, according to their breeders, should never be washed). In tropical or subtropical countries, dog are often bathed weekly to minimize the risk of tick-borne diseases. Dried mud falls off short-coated breeds easily, but a bath will get rid of lingering odours.

Larger dogs can be washed in the bath (put down a rubber mat to stop the dog from slipping), but it is probably better to use an old baby bath and also less messy if you bathe your dog outside. Use warm (not hot) water and either baby shampoo or a medicated shampoo rather than any type of detergent. Special dog shampoos are also available: medicated shampoo, anti-parasitic shampoo, and varieties prescribed by vets to treat specific skin conditions. Try to make the experience fun – and wear something waterproof.

Beginning with the hindquarters, lather the coat well and gently massage the dog, working forwards along the body and trying to make sure that the bubbles do not enter any orifices, especially the eyes. Rinse the dog thoroughly, working from the head backwards, and paying particular attention to the area between the forelegs and hind legs, where shampoo may remain and cause irritation.

After you've bathed it, your dog will probably want to have a vigorous shake, but try to dry it first. Use a chamois leather and a towel to dry short-coated breeds. Long-haired dogs must be dried with a towel using a squeezing motion because rubbing tends to mat the coat. Terriers usually enjoy a rub with a rough towel, and dachshunds and other short-legged dogs are liable to develop colds if their stomachs become cold, making drying them especially important. Follow this rough-drying with a blast of air from a hairdryer on a low setting, but remember that your dog may be startled by the hairdryer if it is not used to it, so introduce its use gradually. Once dry, your dog will look great, but don't be surprised if it immediately rolls around on the ground to cover itself in some familiar smells!

health
THE SIGNS OF A HEALTHY DOG

Most dogs are hardy and healthy, keen-eyed, and bushy of tail. Check the following vital areas, and if your dog does not exhibit the points noted, consult your vet.

- Abdomen: tapering towards the back legs; neither sensitive to touch nor distended.
- Anus: clean.
- Appetite: hearty, fast eater.
- Breathing: quiet and even when at rest; panting when cooling down; no coughing.
- Claws: no splits or interdigital cysts; well trimmed.
- Coat: clean and glossy; no loose hair, dirt, or parasites.
- Ears: clean, no dark wax, no redness; held at correct angle for breed; alert.

- Eyes: clear, no discharge.
- Faeces: varies according to diet, but bowel motions should be regular and reasonably solid.
- Manner: alert; quick response to sounds and instructions.
- Movement: even gait; even weight distribution over all four legs.
- Nose: cold and damp on a walk, dry and warm inside; no discharge.
- Skin: supple, clean, and free from inflammation or sores.
- Teeth: clean and strong; pink gums.
- Urine: passed easily.

neutering

The advantages of neutering far outweigh the disadvantages, and it is notable that all dogs bred as guide dogs in Britain are neutered at the age of six months to ensure that they are stable, peaceable animals. The coats of some breeds become fluffy rather than silky after neutering, which is an aesthetic shame for Irish setters or cocker spaniels. More seriously, a bitch may develop urinary incontinence in later life, but hormone-replacement therapy usually solves this problem. Owners are often worried that neutering their dogs will cause them to put on weight, but if a dog is fed properly, this will not happen. Owners may give their neutered pets more food out of guilt, but studies have shown that neutered dogs have lower calorie requirements (up to 15 percent less) than unneutered animals, so if they are given smaller amounts of food they will not put on weight.

Dogs become sexually mature between six and twelve months of age, although in many cases they are not mentally mature until eighteen months. This means that a young bitch who has a litter when she is still under a year old may find it hard to cope with the demands of motherhood. (In Britain, it is illegal for breeders to breed from such a young animal.) Most owners do not want to breed from their bitches and so have three choices: spaying, controlling the dog's activities during her "seasons," or using hormonal birth-control drugs.

Most bitches come into season every six to nine months throughout their lives. An average season lasts between fifteen and twenty-one days, and most bitches suffer from abdominal pain and moodiness.

PUPPIES ARE SWEET, BUT DO YOU WANT A HOUSE FULL OF THEM?

Unless she actually does become pregnant, a season is followed by a false pregnancy, when the bitch will display signs of pregnancy and maternal behaviour, as well as restlessness. Spaying, which is carried out under general anaesthetic, eliminates these problems and will make your dog more stable.

Most male pet dogs are castrated, an operation that is carried out by a vet using a general anaesthetic. Unneutered males may exhibit behavioural problems, such as mounting people or furniture, aggression, and straying in search of an oestrous female, caused by an increase in testosterone. Castration can be carried out at any age, but it is probably best for the dog to be aged between nine and eighteen months.

breeding

Deciding whether or not to breed from your female dog is an important decision. Consider what you would do with the puppies – and remember the scenes from *A Hundred and One Dalmatians*! It is unlikely that you will want to keep them all, so think about what will happen to them. Will you be able to sell them or give them away? Or will you be left with four or five rapidly growing puppies that will exhaust both your energy and your cash? It is irresponsible to allow your dog to breed if the future of the puppies is uncertain. It is cruel to send them to unsuitable homes, and although rescue centers will look after them more than adequately, their resources are not infinite.

MOST BITCHES REQUIRE LITTLE HELP WHEN WHELPING.

Remember that if you own a crossbreed, the chances of the puppies looking like their mother are reasonably small, and that if both parents have mixed ancestry, it is almost impossible to predict what the puppies will look like. If you are the owner of a purebred dog, however, mating it with another dog of the same breed will at least produce puppies whose looks and behaviour will be predictable. Purchasers of purebred puppies want the best, so try to ensure that the chosen mate has shown its quality, is of sound temperament, and has the relevant Kennel Club and breed certificates.

If you feel that you have the necessary resources to breed from your female dog, contact your vet, who will be able to suggest a reputable breeder (to help you to find a prospective mate) and will advise you on how to care for her during pregnancy.

MATING

A bitch's season usually lasts about three weeks. Her vulva swells and there will be a blood-stained discharge; male dogs (although not humans) will be able to detect a powerful odour signifying that she is in season. She is fertile about twelve days from the first signs of coming into season and remains so for about five to seven

A CHOCOLATE-BROWN BUNDLE OF FUN AND MISCHIEF.

days. This is the time to mate her with a suitable sire – and male dogs are always ready to mate! Do not breed from a bitch until she is at least two years old because she will not be physically or mentally mature enough to cope with motherhood properly until then.

Pregnancy lasts for sixty-three days, but is hard to spot. After every season, hormonal changes occur (known as a "false pregnancy") whether the bitch is pregnant or not, so no blood or urine tests can confirm the presence of puppies. About six weeks into the pregnancy, the bitch's abdomen will become noticeably fuller and her mammary glands will be enlarged – these are obvious signs of impending motherhood.

The mother-to-be will need extra food and rest from now on. Increase her food gradually until, by the end of her pregnancy, she is eating about two-thirds more than normal, and give her two meals a day. Smaller dogs will probably double their normal diets. A few days before the arrival of the litter, she may lose interest in food and vomit up her last meal.

WHELPING

About two weeks before the puppies are due, prepare a whelping box and introduce your dog to it. It should sited in a warm, quiet spot, but make sure that it is accessible in case you or the vet need to help

MAKE SURE YOU HAVE THE TIME TO DEAL WITH A LITTER.

with whelping. Whelping boxes are sold through pet-supply stores; alternatively, you can make one. Line it with a warm, washable, synthetic fleece and newspaper – whelping is a messy business. Prepare a box of old towels, disinfectant, and scissors and keep it nearby.

Most bitches whelp without difficulty, but it is sensible to talk through the process with your vet in advance. A day or so before the birth, the dog will probably become uninterested in food and very restless, perhaps trying to make a nest somewhere. Shortly before labour starts, the dog will pant and her temperature will drop by two or three degrees (a dog's normal temperature is 100.4°F or 38°C). It may take several hours from the beginning of the contractions until the arrival of the first pup, but once the first has appeared, the remainder should follow at intervals of ten to eighty minutes.

Owners will probably be little more than observers at the birth, but make sure that one placenta is delivered for each pup. If your dog appears to be having an unproductive labour, with lots of straining but no sign of a puppy emerging, contact your vet. She may need a Caesarean, which is relatively common for breeds with large heads, such as bulldogs. Do not let your dog become exhausted by labour because, at the very least, this will impede her recovery.

Puppies are born either head or tail first – either way is normal. The mother will lick the newborn pups vigorously to remove the membranes and will chew through the umbilical cord to separate it from the placenta, which she will later eat. She will continue to lick each puppy to stimulate it, clear away mucus, and warm it.

Once all of the puppies have been delivered, their mother will feed them and lick their bottoms to stimulate the elimination of faeces and urine. She will consume all of the puppies' waste for three weeks (this is a throwback to the behaviour of dogs' wild ancestors, which needed to hide the presence of vulnerable young from predators). For the first three weeks, the puppies are entirely dependent on their mother and will do little more than feed and sleep, huddling together for warmth and security. Their eyes open at about ten days.

Some breeds are prone to cannibalism and will lick their puppies obsessively before taking this process to a natural conclusion and consuming them. Bull terriers are most likely to do this, and a nursing mother must therefore be watched closely until the puppies' umbilical cords have dropped off.

Owners should ensure that the mother is comfortable, warm, healthy, and well fed, which will help her milk production. Handle the puppies, but do not upset their mother, who will be very protective of them. Check that they are all gaining weight by weighing them daily. By four weeks of age they will be more active and learning how to interact with their peers.

Weaning can begin at three weeks, when you will need to supplement the puppies' diet (this will also lessen the strain on their mother). They should be completely weaned at six weeks, when they can be fed on puppy food. Consult your vet about worming and vaccinations. And by the age of eight weeks, the puppies will be ready to leave home.

PROVIDE PRACTICAL HELP FOR AGEING DOGS, SUCH AS THIS RAMP UP TO THE CAR.

older dogs

Given the wide variety of types of dog, it is not surprising that life expectancy varies from breed to breed. Generally, smaller dogs live longer than larger dogs; terriers, for example, may live for as long as twenty years, although miniature dogs are less fortunate. Giant dogs, such as Great Danes, rarely survive beyond the age of ten, while bulldogs average about seven years. The average life expectancy for a crossbreed dog is thirteen years, and most dogs are considered old at the age of seven or eight. One of the most important factors contributing to its longevity is the quality of the care that the dog has received throughout its life. If untreated, illnesses or infections contracted early in life, for instance, may weaken an organ and result in health problems a few years later.

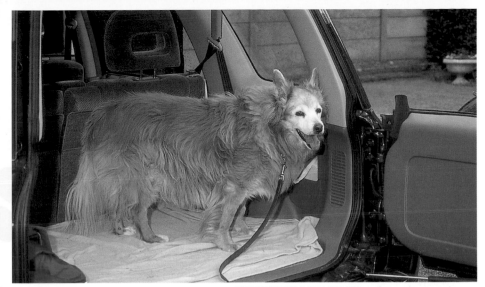

OLDER DOGS WILL LIVE LIFE AT A SLOWER PACE, BUT ARE STILL LIVELY ENOUGH TO ENJOY A CAR RIDE.

OLDER DOGS NEED LESS EXERCISE.

THE ARRIVAL OF A NEW DOG MAY PERK UP AN OLDER ANIMAL.

Certain breeds are prone to particular diseases in old age (see Chapter 7), to which a breeder or vet will certainly alert you when you acquire a dog. Arthritis and incontinence, which afflict many old dogs, can be alleviated by medical treatment. There are many pet-insurance schemes which will help to keep the expense of vets' bills to a minimum, and it is prudent to take out a policy before your dog reaches five years of age.

Older dogs are generally less energetic than younger ones, but the ageing process is gradual, and it is often hard to recognize the signs of ageing until problems occur. Ideally, dogs over seven years of age should have a checkup at the vet's every six months.

The behaviour of older dogs alters subtly over time. They generally sleep more and may become more irritable, especially around exuberant youngsters — human or canine. They sometimes bark more often, which may be a sign of deafness or that something else is troubling the animal. You may need to be flexible in your routines to accommodate the changing needs of your dog. It will probably eat less, for example, and may prefer a couple of smaller meals each day instead of one large one. If your dog has a stiff neck, raise its feeding and drinking bowls to head height. Mobility may become a problem, and joint stiffness may occur in the morning or after exercise. However reluctant your old dog seems, try to make sure that it is well exercised to keep its joints mobile, stimulate its mind, and improve its bowel function. Frequent short walks are probably easier for an old dog to manage than long ones, particularly if it is suffering from heart, respiratory, or arthritic problems.

Your dog may become upset and confused by its ageing body, as well as frustrated that it can no longer do the things it used to. Try to avoid inflicting stressful situations on an older dog. Routine and familiarity are more important than ever, so try not to make any sudden changes to the dog's circumstances.

AGE-RELATED
HEALTH PROBLEMS

- Tumours and benign growths: if you spot one, consult the vet immediately.
- Heart: your dog may be reluctant to exercise and may be prone to coughing after lying down for long periods.
- Teeth: dental disease is common in dogs aged over three years old. Brush your dog's teeth daily (see page 157) and consult your vet at the first sign of trouble. If left untreated, dental disease can affect a dog's overall health.
- Anal sacs: if your dog has a habit of dragging its bottom along the floor, its anal sacs probably need emptying. Consult the vet.
- Nails: nails will require clipping more frequently if they are not being kept short by exercise.
- Incontinence: poor bladder control is relatively common in older dogs. Make sure that the dog has waterproof bedding in a bed that is easy to clean. Don't punish your dog for any accidents – it really can't help it.

- Obesity: old dogs may put on weight if they take less exercise. Regulate your dog's diet to avoid obesity, which can lead to more serious health problems.
- Hearing: if your dog's hearing begins to decline, it will not be able to hear certain frequencies. Because it may not hear your voice clearly, non-compliance with commands may not be disobedience, merely the result of deafness. Because it may not be able to hear traffic noise, ensure that it is kept on a leash near roads. Check its ears for infection or a build-up of wax.
- Eyes: eyes may appear cloudy, which could be a sign of cataracts. If your dog shows signs of deteriorating vision, try to avoid repositioning any furniture within the house and do not let it off the leash when out walking.
- Coat: the coat will probably become flecked with gray and feel coarser.

OLD HABITS DIE HARD – THIS AGEING DOG IS STILL AN ALERT GUARD DOG.

caring for your dog

THE LAST KINDNESS

If your dog has a physical problem or disease that considerably reduces its quality of life, or if it is in constant pain, your vet will advise you on the most humane course of action. Consider what your dog can still do and whether it seems happy. Is it able to walk and feed itself, for example, and is it continent? Confronting death is hard, but if your pet is suffering, ending its pain is the greatest kindness that you can bestow on it.

SEVEN

disorders and illnesses

AN ALERT PAIR LISTEN TO THEIR OWNER.

It is unlikely that your dog will cruise through life without incurring any health problems. This section offers guidance on how to spot signs of trouble, how to prevent some common illnesses or infections, and how to look after a sick dog. If your dog's behaviour alters dramatically, for example, if it rejects its food or the frequency with which it empties its bowels or bladder changes, consult your vet.

Your dog is far more likely to remain healthy if it is given basic inoculations as a puppy (see page 105). These will protect it against common, but unpleasant, and potentially fatal, diseases. Boosters are usually given annually, and it is vital that your dog receives them to maintain its immunity. Preventative medicine is a crucial part of canine healthcare. Distemper vaccinations must be boosted every other year to maintain immunity, and leptospirosis vaccinations, which only give short-lived protection, more regularly. Kennel cough, which is caused by several infectious agents and is transmitted through fairly close contact between dogs, can be prevented by a nasal-spray vaccine, which wards off most, if not all, components of the infection. Most kennels advise owners to treat their dogs before installing them in kennels for any length of time.

Your vet will become an important partner in maintaining your dog's health, so it is important that you find one with whom you feel comfortable. Ask friends for their recommendations or, if it seems adequate, simply register with the practice nearest to your home. Check the facilities, opening times, and appointment system, and make sure that you keep the phone number in a prominent place in case you need it urgently. Veterinary advice and treatment does not come cheap, and new dog-owners will be well advised to take out a suitable insurance policy. These vary tremendously in terms of their cost and coverage: the most expensive policies will pay out in the event of your dog's death, but others are far more limited with regard to which illnesses or treatments they will pay for. Do a little research to find the best policy for your circumstances – your vet may be able to advise you.

IF YOUR DOG SEEMS OFF-COLOUR, TAKE IT TO THE VET.

inherited diseases

In the wild, only the fittest survive, which means that inherited diseases are a relatively minor problem. However, the dog, which has been domesticated and selectively bred for so long, is prone to more inherited disorders than any other species of animal apart from humans. Inherited diseases are passed from one generation to the next through the affected genes of the sire or dam – and sometimes from both. Even healthy dogs can pass on a problem if they carry a recessive gene.

Large breeds, such as German shepherds, retrievers, and Great Danes, are prone to degenerative hip dysplasia, which causes pain and lameness in the hind legs. It can be treated with medication, but surgery is necessary in severe cases. Progressive retinal atrophy, an eye disease which leads to blindness, can be a problem for Irish setters, cocker spaniels, collies, and retrievers, while Dalmatians may suffer from hereditary deafness.

Breeders have begun to cooperate to eliminate genetic diseases from some breeds. Progressive retinal atrophy, for example, has a straightforward inheritance pattern, and Irish setter breeders have worked to reduce the occurrence of the condition in the breed. Progress is slow, however, because eliminating affected

ROUGH COLLIES ARE PRONE TO PROGRESSIVE RETINAL ATROPHY, A SERIOUS VISUAL DISORDER.

IRISH SETTERS MAY SUFFER FROM VISUAL DEFECTS.

AMERICAN COCKER SPANIELS OFTEN SUFFER FROM EPILEPSY.

dogs from breeding programmes is only part of the solution. Other diseases, such as hip dysplasia, are hard to eliminate because they sometimes do not manifest themselves until relatively late in a dog's life, and certainly beyond the prime breeding age. As scientists learn more about genetics and the canine genome, it is likely that DNA tests will become available to pinpoint genetic diseases and, in time, eliminate them.

diseases shared with humans: zoonoses

There are a number of diseases (known as zoonoses) and parasites that spread from dogs to humans, but most can be combated with a stringent routine of basic hygiene.

Regular deworming and the removal of dog faeces from the environment are especially important to prevent the transmission of the Toxocara canis roundworm eggs that can survive in soil for up to two years. Children are most susceptible to worms, so make sure that they do not come into contact with dog feces when playing in parks, and do not allow dogs to lick their faces. Encourage children to

CHILDREN AND DOGS MUST RESPECT EACH OTHER.

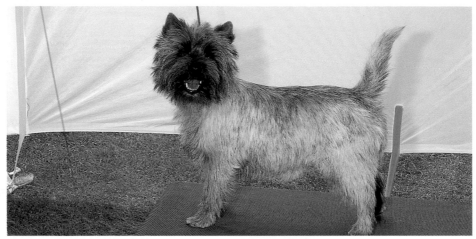

TERRIERS, LIKE THE CAIRN VARIETY SHOWN HERE, ARE PARTICULARY PRONE TO LEPTOSPIROSIS

wash their hands after they have played with a dog before a meal, too. If infectious Toxocara roundworm larva are swallowed by humans, they can produce allergic reactions and, in extreme cases, blindness. (See page 200 for details of worming treatments.)

Ringworm infections cause circular skin lesions in humans and should be treated by a doctor, while flea and tick bites irritate human skin and transfer diseases like Lyme disease.

Rabies, a potentially fatal disease, is transmitted in saliva, usually via bite wounds. It exists almost everywhere in the world apart from a few islands and peninsulas, among them Britain, Australia, Scandinavia, and the islands of the Caribbean. All mammals are susceptible to rabies, but it is commonly carried by foxes, raccoons, mongooses, bats, skunks, cats, and dogs. In Africa and Asia, dogs are the usual source of infection, and it is foolhardy to handle a stray dog in these regions, but if you are bitten, immediately seek medical advice about being given the rabies anti-serum. An infected dog is usually aggressive and salivates a great deal (although foaming at the mouth is an exaggeration).

Leptospirosis exists in two forms, one of which is linked to rats, which means that terriers are particularly prone to it, especially on farms, where they may encounter the bacterium via rats' urine. (It can be transferred to humans as Weil's disease.) A farm dog could also infect another animal. The second form, *Leptospira icterohaemorrhagiae*, leads to jaundice, and early symptoms include diarrhoea, vomiting, and fever. Antibiotics usually clear it up and it can also be prevented via vaccination. In the later stages of the illness, an infected dog may appear permanently thirsty and experience breathing difficulties.

how to spot signs of illness

Most owners know their dogs well enough to spot the signs of illness. Poorly dogs may not behave in their normal manner, perhaps appearing listless, declining food, or drinking prodigious quantities of water. Weight loss over several weeks may indicate illness, while slowly developing swellings may be the beginning of some sort of tumour (not necessarily cancerous). Hair loss, skin problems, slight lameness, and occasional vomiting are also signs that something is not quite right.

Daily grooming is a chance for you to check your dog's health and also accustoms your pet to being handled. Check your dog carefully using this checklist.

- Are its eyes bright and clean? Sores, discharge, or ulcers should not be present.

- Is its nose clean, slightly moist, and free from crusty discharge?

- Check your dog's mouth to ensure that it looks pink. The gums should be pink (but are sometimes naturally mottled with black), the teeth should not be discoloured, and there should be no foreign bodies or traces of food in the mouth.

- Are its ears clean and free from waxy discharge or odour?

GROOMING ENABLES YOU TO CHECK A DOG'S HEALTH.

- Check its paws for cuts, abrasions, and foreign bodies trapped between the toes.

- Is your dog scratching or worrying at part of its body?

- Does your dog appear lame? Sometimes lameness is obvious, but in other cases it is manifested by changes in the dog's posture or a subtle alteration in its gait.

- Does it have a raised temperature? A normal canine temperature ranges between 100.4 and 102.2°F (38 and 39°C).

If you are concerned about your dog's health, write down the symptoms and note how long they have lasted – these details will help the vet to diagnose the dog's problem.

GROOMING IS AN IDEAL TIME TO CHECK FOR ANY SIGNS OF ILL HEALTH

call the vet ...

... if you are in any doubt about your dog's health. Medical intervention is vital if your dog collapses, appears unable to breathe, loses consciousness, or has convulsions. If your dog has been injured, is bleeding profusely, has been scalded, poisoned or is in danger of drowning, or is having difficulties whelping, get veterinary attention as quickly as possible.

Other potentially serious problems include the following.

• A swollen stomach that is obviously tender, accompanied by panting and salivation. This may be bloat or gastric torsion and is an emergency situation.

• Vomiting: if this persists for more than twelve hours, consult a vet.

• Diarrhoea lasting for more than twenty-four hours or blood-stained faeces require veterinary treatment.

• Breathing difficulties, gasping, or choking require medical help.

• Collapse or unconsciousness require immediate veterinary attention.

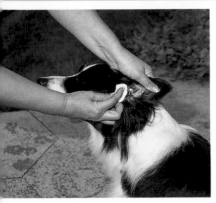

CKING EARS FOR INFECTION.

SERIOUS PROBLEMS MAY NEED SURGICAL INTERVENTION.

administering medicine

1 Tablets can be crushed and disguised within food, but if you need to be absolutely certain that your dog has swallowed its medication, you must place the tablet at the back of the dog's mouth.

2 Do this by holding the muzzle with one hand while tilting the head slightly upward. Grasp the lower jaw with your other hand and use your index finger and thumb to place the pill on the dog's tongue as far back as possible.

3 Hold the mouth shut and gently massage the throat to encourage the dog to swallow the tablet.

4 Liquid medicine is most easily given by using a plastic syringe to shoot the medicine to the back of the dog's mouth. A syringe enables you measure the quantity precisely, and if you pipe the medicine in steadily, the dog will swallow it reasonably easily. Wash the syringe afterwards and reward your dog for its good behaviour. Eye drops can be administered by holding the dog's head steady (you may need an assistant) and tipping it slightly backwards. Apply the drops to the corner of the eye.

disorders

actually damage the eye. Discharges are the most common form of eye complaint, but more serious problems are harder to spot. If you are in the least worried by your dog's vision or eyes, consult a vet.

EYES

Dogs' eyes are very expressive, and because eye contact is an important dog–human form of communication, owners are usually quick to notice any ocular problems. A dog may try to scratch its eye with its paw if there is an irritant in it, which may

Clear Discharge

Tears, or clear discharge, are usually produced to wash away irritants. If the tear duct is blocked by mucus or an infection, tears can overflow and run down the face, which, if prolonged, can stain the fur.

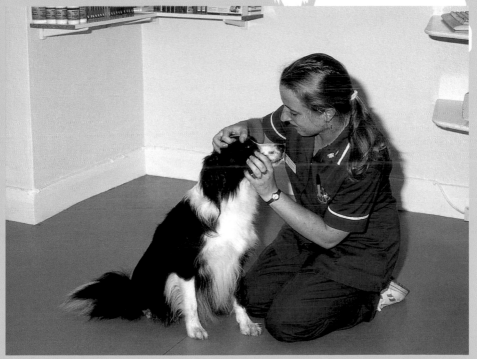

A VET CHECKS A DOG'S EYES FOR DISCHARGE, REDNESS, OR INFLAMMATION.

Light-coloured dogs, such as poodles, often display brown fur around their eyes, the result of "poodle eye," or blocked tear ducts. If left untreated, surgical intervention may be necessary to clear the blocked duct. Excessive tears may also be a symptom of another problem, so always consult your vet.

Dry Eye

Insufficient tear production may lead to dry eye, or *Keratoconjunctivitis sicca*, in which the eyeball's normal, healthy moistness is replaced by a sticky discharge and inflammation. This is most common in older dogs and can lead to blindness, but your vet can treat it with antibiotics and eye-drops.

Cloudy or Inflamed Eyes

Keratitis, a severe inflammation of the cornea or outer-eye surface caused by injury or infectious disease, must be treated by a vet. The cloudy, blue-gray cornea caused by Keratitis should not be confused with blue eye, a condition usually associated with a specific viral infection like hepatitis (in most cases, the eye recovers within a few days). Cataracts also cause cloudiness within the eye, and although they are associated with other eye diseases, they are more usually a problem of old age. Cataracts cause a deterioration in vision and can be removed if a vet thinks that the operation will result in an improvement in the dog's sight.

Visual Problems

Visual problems are hard to spot and diagnose until a dog begins to bump into furniture, at which point you should seek professional help. Some breeds are more likely to suffer from inherited eye disorders. Collie eye anomaly, for example, is the faulty development of the retina that occurs in rough and smooth collies and produces visual defects ranging from mild short-sightedness to total blindness.

Progressive Retinal Atrophy

Progressive retinal atrophy (RPA) first manifests itself as night-blindness, but may not be apparent until the dog begins to bump into things. Although it is an inherited and incurable condition, many blind dogs live contented and fulfilled lives.

EARS

Most dogs shake their heads on waking, but persistent head-shaking, ear-scratching, or signs of discharge indicate an ear problem. Dogs with long, floppy, hairy ears, such as spaniels, are more prone to ear diseases than those with erect ears, and their ears should be cleaned regularly. The insides of healthy ears look shiny and pale pink and are free from wax and odour. Do not insert anything into your dog's ears with which to clean out wax unless you are certain that there is no underlying problem.

EARS MUST BE KEPT CLEAN. CHECK FOR EAR-MITE INFESTATION, EXCESSIVE WAX, OR INFLAMMATION.

Ear-mite Infestations

Ear-mite infestations are common in puppies and spread quickly from dog to dog, irritating the lining of the ear and increasing the production of wax. A vet will prescribe insecticidal ear drops to treat the problem.

Inflammation

Grass seeds often cause inflammation in spaniels' ears, and the first sign of such a problem is often excessive shaking of the head as the dog tries to dislodge the foreign body. A vet will probably remove the source of irritation with forceps and administer anti-inflammatory drops to restore the ear to health.

Inner-ear Infection

If your dog exhibits problems in balancing, such as appearing unsteady on its paws and tilting its head in the direction of one ear, it may have an inner-ear infection. Antibiotics usually solve the problem, although the infected ear may need to be drained by a vet. It is also sensible to restrict your dog's movements while it appears wobbly.

A DOG HAS ITS TEETH CLEANED BY THE VET.

ORAL DISORDERS

Gum Disease

Gum disease, or gingivitis, affects over 70 percent of adult dogs and is caused by bacteria breeding in the remnants of food trapped between the teeth. Gum disease can be prevented by rigorous dental hygiene, that is, cleaning your dog's teeth every day (see page 157). The first sign of this condition is often bad breath followed by sore, inflamed gums, and if it is untreated, it will lead to tooth decay.

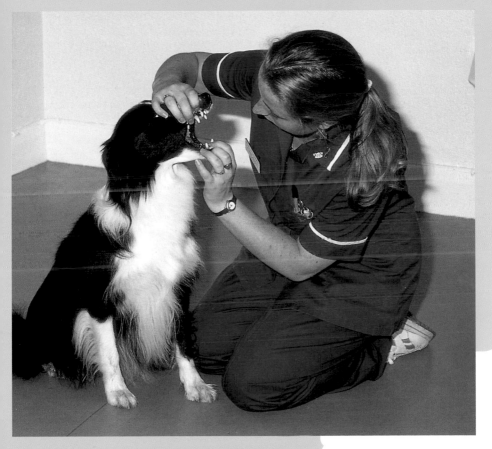

TEETH AND GUMS MUST BE REGULARLY CHECKED FOR GINGIVITIS AND TOOTH DECAY.

Excessive Drooling

Excessive drooling may be caused by a cyst on a salivary gland. Such cysts look like blisters and usually appear under the tongue, but also develop under the skin in the neck by the jaw. Consult your vet, who will probably drain the cyst and remove the salivary gland.

EXTERNAL PARASITES

Fleas afflict nearly every dog at some point in their lives and flourish in warm environments. They are not immediately visible unless they are present in large numbers, but you may see flecks of reddish-brown dirt, the traces of blood that are left behind after fleas have bitten their host. Fleas move swiftly through a dog's coat and are extremely difficult to catch, although special combs help to sweep them out. If you place the specks of dirt on a piece of white tissue paper and find that the traces of blood stain the paper red, this confirms the presence of fleas.

A female flea lays her eggs on the floor or in bedding. After a week, the eggs hatch into larvae, which mature within two or three weeks. Because fleas can live in carpets and bedding, once you have treated the dog, vacuum its bedding and the surrounding area and apply a biological spray to kill any surviving fleas. If any remain, they will breed and reinfect the dog. Fleas also act as hosts for the larvae of the common tapeworm

(see next page), making it doubly important to treat an infestation. Ask your vet for an insecticide which will kill the fleas and prevent the eggs from hatching.

Mange mites and lice are usually caught from other dogs. Demodex mange mites live deep within the hair follicles, particularly of short-coated breeds. Invisible to the naked eye, they mainly afflict young puppies and elderly, infirm dogs. They can be treated by bathing your dog once a week in a special insecticide. Demodetic mange is more unsightly than irritating, but the affected areas often become infected, the skin may thicken and become wrinkly, like elephant hide, and pustules may form. If left untreated, hair follicles may be destroyed and, in severe cases, any skin changes may become permanent.

Sarcoptes mites can invade a dog's ear tips and elbows by burrowing into the skin, causing these sites to become itchy and scabby. (They can inflict itchy, mosquito-like bites on humans, too). Infested dogs must be bathed weekly for at least four weeks to kill the parasites.

Harvest mites, or chiggers, only infest dogs during their larval stage during the fall, when they usually attach themselves to dogs' paws, causing severe irritation. Insecticidal shampoo usually kills them, although anti-inflammatory medicine may also be necessary.

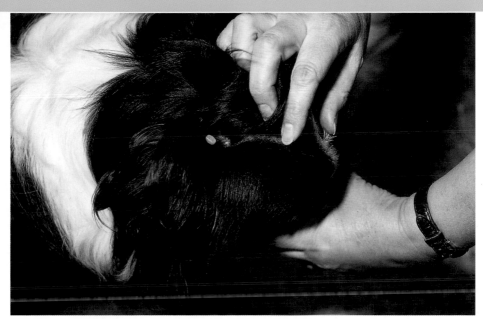

PARASITES INFEST MOST DOGS AT SOME POINT. A TICK HAS SET UP HOME ON THIS ANIMAL.

FLEA AND TICK INFESTATIONS CAN BE TREATED WITH SPRAYS, POWDERS, AND TABLETS.

INTERNAL PARASITES

All dogs lick their bottoms, but constant licking of the anal region or dragging the bottom along the ground can be signs that your dog is infected with worms. The two most common worms in dogs are roundworms and tapeworms.

Roundworms (*Toxocara canis* or *Toxocaris leonina*) infect most puppies, partly because they are transmitted from dog to dog via faecal contamination. The larvae can also be transmitted from a mother to her unborn puppies, which means that puppies may have mature worms within them at the age of only two weeks. Infected puppies may appear pot-bellied and will gain weight only slowly. Most breeders will treat the entire litter with worming medicine at the age of three or four weeks, and the treatment should be repeated every month or so until the dogs are six months old. Your vet will advise you on the best course of treatment, but it is sensible to worm adult dogs every three months because roundworms also pose a hazard to human health.

Tapeworms are more common in older dogs than in puppies and have a life cycle based upon two hosts: the dog and its fleas. It is hard to know when tapeworms are present, the only sign being small "rice grains" (the tapeworms' dried egg sacs) around the dog's anus and in its faeces. Treatment is usually a medicine prescribed by the vet, but prevention, as they say, is better than cure, and this depends on controlling the flea problem. Never allow your dog to eat animal carcasses or offal from animals such as sheep because both are sources of tapeworm infection.

Dogs living in unhygienic conditions are susceptible to other species of worm, too, such as whipworms and hookworms, both of which live within the intestine and can cause diarrhoea, while hookworms can result in serious bleeding and anemia in the host dog. Veterinary treatment is vital in both cases.

COMMON AILMENTS OF THE NERVOUS SYSTEM

Diseases of the nervous system are often caused by viruses, such as rabies or distemper, and viral damage can lead to paralysis, behavioural changes, loss of balance, or seizures. Viruses or bacterial infections may inflame the lining of the brain, while head injuries resulting in damaged brain tissue may cause epilepsy.

Chorea

Chorea, or involuntary muscle-twitching, is usually a symptom of another disease, such as distemper. It often begins a couple of weeks after apparent recovery from the disease and is most noticeable when the dog is asleep. Because it can progress to cause major muscle spasms and then convulsions, veterinary advice is vital.

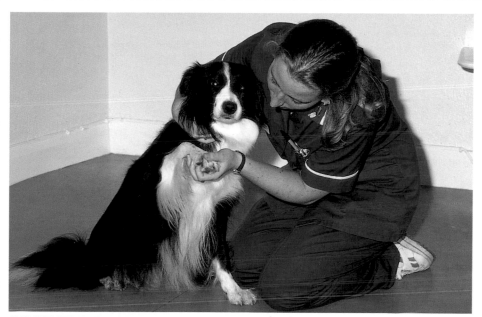

GRASS SEEDS OFTEN CAUSE INFECTION IF THEY BECOME TRAPPED IN A DOG'S SOFT PAW PAD.

CHOREA IS MOST NOTICEABLE WHEN THE DOG IS ASLEEP.

Distemper and Hard Pad

Although the majority of puppies are inoculated against distemper, some still catch this miserable illness. Highly infectious, and sometimes fatal, it usually afflicts young dogs. The classic signs are thick discharge from the nose and eyes, forming a crusty residue, persistent coughing, fever, vomiting, and diarrhea. It can lead to encephalitis (inflammation of the brain) and fits, but, with good care, most dogs recover. Hard pad occurs when the virus affects the horny layer of the dog's paws, making them feel leathery. Veterinary intervention is vital.

Loss of Balance

Loss of balance may be a sign of an inner-ear infection (see page 197), when the dog may cock its head quite obviously towards the affected side. An inner-ear infection can be treated with antibiotics.

Rabies

Although behavioural changes are sometimes prompted by neurological problems, rabies is the most serious cause (but this disease has currently been eradicated from Britain). The first sign is often a change of temperament: gentle dogs become more aggressive and active dogs quieter. As the disease progresses over the course of about ten days, gradual paralysis sets in and the dog eventually dies from respiratory failure.

Seizures

Seizures can be controlled by drugs, but may be a sign of another problem, such as encephalitis, epilepsy, or a brain tumour. Encephalitis can be treated with antibiotics, and tumours can sometimes be removed from the brain. Whatever the cause, consult a vet if your dog has a convulsion.

DIGESTIVE AILMENTS

Dogs are natural scavengers, and if they are allowed to grab food at any opportunity, they will inevitably become ill. Some dogs eat grass regularly and others do it sporadically to ease abdominal discomfort because it usually provokes vomiting. Persistent vomiting, or vomiting blood or bile, are signs of a serious problem, however, as is persistent diarrhoea.

If your dog has vomited, do not give it any solid food for a day, but allow it unlimited access to water. If, after twenty-four hours, it is still vomiting, take it to the vet's. Severe vomiting may caused by gastric torsion, a life-threatening condition, or an infection, such as canine parvovirus. (Puppies are inoculated against canine parvovirus, but this infectious, potentially fatal, virus may still take hold, manifesting itself as chronic vomiting and blood-stained diarrhoea). In both instances, seek veterinary help.

Loss of appetite may also indicate that your dog is not well.

Constipation

The consistency of dogs' motions, and the frequency with which they are passed, vary, but constipation is obvious when a dog has difficulty passing stools, straining or showing other signs of discomfort.

Constipation is more usually a problem in ageing dogs than in young ones, when it is often a symptom of poor gut motility. It may also be a sign of blocked anal sacs, which, although they can be squeezed to empty them, may require antibiotic treatment. Ingested bones also cause digestive troubles.

Dogs sometimes produce greasy motions when they have difficulty digesting fat (which may be a sign of pancreatic failure), and if this is the case, avoid giving your dog an oily laxative. Otherwise, ask your vet's advice for a suitable laxative, such as liquid paraffin.

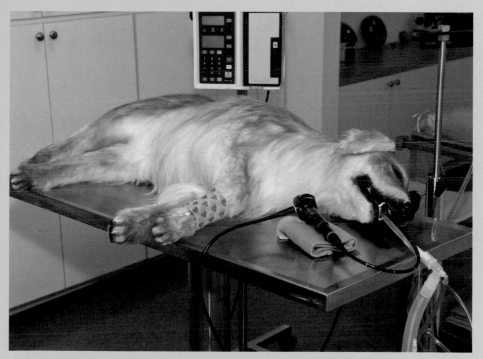

A DOG IS ANAESTHETIZED PRIOR TO SURGERY.

Gastric Distension, Bloat, or Gastric Torsion

Gastric distension (also known as bloat or gastric torsion) usually affects large dogs, such as Great Danes, although it can also occur in Pekingese and dachshunds. The dog may show obvious signs of pain two to four hours after feeding, the abdomen may appear distended and hard, and the dog may also try to vomit. This is a surgical emergency, so get veterinary help immediately.

Weight Problems

If your dog suddenly develops a voracious appetite and great thirst and also steadily loses weight, ask your vet to test it for diabetes. In most cases, diabetes can be treated with daily injections of insulin to control the dog's blood-sugar level.

Equally, if your dog becomes lethargic and starts to put on weight when you have made no changes to its diet, consult your vet because an underactive thyroid gland may be slowing down its metabolism. This problem is easily treatable with drugs.

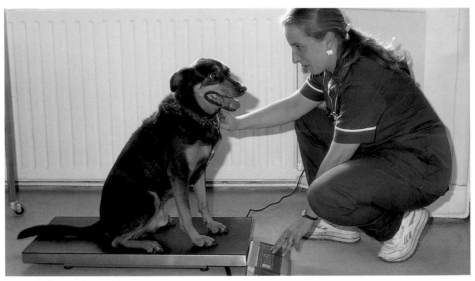

EXCESSIVE WEIGHT GAIN OR WEIGHT LOSS MAY BE A SIGN OF ILLNESS.

In most cases, however, weight gain is the result of lack of exercise and over-feeding. Try not to let your dog become overweight – obese dogs have a shorter life expectancy and, in some cases, a poorer quality of life than slim ones.

Urinary Problems

Any change in your dog's ability to urinate, or frequency of urination, should be investigated by a vet.

If your dog appears to strain to urinate, it may be a sign of a bladder infection or of stones, which can lodge in the urinary system anywhere from the kidneys through the urethra to the bladder. Dogs with bladder stones usually urinate frequently in small amounts because they are unable to empty their bladder properly. If the problem is caused by an infection, antibiotics will usually relieve it. If there is a serious blockage, however, the vet may use a catheter to empty the bladder. Bladder stones are visible on X-rays and, in many cases, can be treated using dietary changes.

Incontinence is reasonably common in older dogs, who are usually unaware of leaking urine. It also occurs in younger dogs, usually in spayed females, when it is caused by a hormonal imbalance that can be treated with a hormone spray. Male dogs may experience similar problems when they have an enlarged prostate gland.

An increase in the frequency of urination may be caused by a bladder or kidney infection, or possibly by diabetes or a liver problem. Consult a vet, who will probably want to take a urine sample for analysis.

Kidney disease (rather than merely an infection) is often a cause of serious illness in adult dogs. Acute kidney failure usually manifests itself as fever, increased thirst, and decreased urination, the urine itself being dark in colour and almost sticky. Immediate veterinary attention is necessary to administer fluids intravenously.

CIRCULATORY AND RESPIRATORY PROBLEMS

Although blood disorders are rare in dogs, heart disease is almost as common in dogs as in humans. Sudden heart failure is unusual, but is more common in large breeds, such as the Doberman. Some breeds are prone to progressive valvular heart disease, particularly King Charles spaniels. Heart conditions can be treated with drugs and careful monitoring of the dog's lifestyle – exercise is vital.

Coughing is usually an attempt to dislodge mucus or foreign bodies from the respiratory system, but it may be a symptom of a more serious disease, such as distemper or kennel cough. Kennel cough is a rasping, unproductive cough that often occurs in dogs that have recently returned from a stay in kennels. The dog may not appear particularly ill, but the cough is caused by the Bordetella bacterium, and secondary infection can lead to pneumonia. It is sensible to vaccinate your dog against kennel cough prior to a stay in kennels.

A moist cough, sometimes known as "heart cough," may be a sign of circulatory problems and occurs after exercise, usually in older dogs. Any persistent cough requires veterinary treatment, particularly if it is accompanied by a refusal to eat or any sign of distress.

EXTERNAL DISORDERS
Anal Sacs

Anal sacs are two pockets, one on each side of the anus, containing glands that produce the pungent secretions used by dogs to communicate scent-marking and whether a bitch is in oestrus. Dogs occasionally empty their anal sacs involuntarily in stressful situations. If the anal sacs become blocked, they will first cause irritation and then pain, and an affected dog may drag its behind along the ground. (It is easy to confuse this behaviour with the symptoms of fleas or worms.) Although evacuation of the anal sacs is relatively

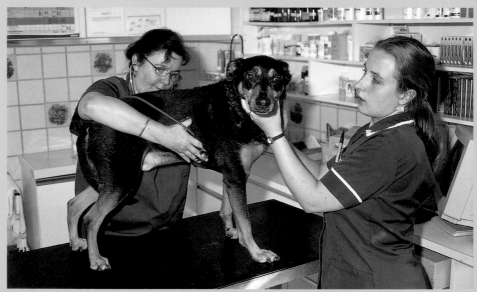

A VET USES A STETHOSCOPE TO CHECK THIS ELDERLY DOG'S HEART RATE.

simple, it is best to ask a vet to do it because the cause of the problem needs to be diagnosed.

Lick Granuloma

Lick granuloma usually occurs on the fore leg (often in Labradors and short-hared dogs), when a small cut or abrasion is opened up by the constant licking of a bored dog and does not heal properly. The skin becomes itchy and eventually ulcerates. Bandaging the leg sometimes prevents licking, but the best cure is to fit a funnel-shaped "Elizabethan collar" around your dog's neck to prevent it licking itself.

AN "ELIZABETHAN COLLAR" TO PREVENT SCRATCHING.

although terriers are also affected. Dry seborrhoea looks like dandruff, and both types are easily treated with an anti-sebum shampoo. Seborrhoea is caused by parasites, a yeast infection, a hormonal imbalance or poor diet.

SKIN AND COAT DISORDERS

Skin conditions are among the most common and irritating problems to afflict dogs. Scratching is usually a sign of fleas or other parasites, but incessant scratching can aggravate the problem by causing further inflammation and irritation and damaging the skin.

Seborrhoea

Seborrhoea, or an overproduction of the sebum, produced by the sebaceous glands, that lubricates the skin, produces a dull, greasy coat with a mouse-like smell. It is most common in cocker spaniels,

Hair Loss

Hair-loss patterns vary from breed to breed and, indeed, from dog to dog. Some breeds shed their hair almost perpetually, especially in spring and fall, when a new coat grows. However, some dogs shed excessive amounts of hair without it thinning the coat, which is probably the result of a hormonal imbalance or possibly environmental factors, such as central heating. Frequent grooming is vital, both to maintain a healthy coat and to prevent itchiness.

Localized hair loss may be caused by ringworm (see page 189) or parasites, such as mange mites (see page 200), both of which are easily treated. In some breeds – particularly collies – sunburn can lead to hair loss on the muzzle, and vulnerable dogs must be protected by a high-factor sun cream. Other dogs suffer hair loss on the elbows, which is simply caused by too much pressure being applied to hard surfaces. Calluses may also develop, but a moisturizing cream will help to combat this problem, while soft bedding will minimize any discomfort.

Warts, Cysts, and Tumours

Warts are common in older dogs of most breeds, especially spaniels and poodles. They can become infected, at which point your vet may advise their surgical removal. Cysts feel like hard lumps under the skin, whereas tumors, which are usually benign and affect older dogs, can be felt as soft, fluctuating masses beneath the skin.

REPRODUCTIVE DISORDERS

Many reproductive disorders, such as womb infections in females, can be avoided by having your dog neutered (see page 168). All sexually active dogs should be checked for sexually transmitted diseases, such as brucellosis, which can cause infertility.

Prostate disease, in which the prostate gland becomes enlarged, is a problem of older male dogs. The prostate gland is sited by the exit to the bladder and underneath the rectum, so the first sign of trouble may be urinary incontinence and/or constipation (because the swollen gland obstructs the rectum). Some cases may be treated either by hormonal drugs or castration.

EXCESSIVE SCRATCHING MAY BE A SIGN OF FLEAS.

SOME SMOOTH COLLIES SUFFER FROM DEAFNESS.

MINIATURE POODLES MAY ENDURE BONE DISORDERS.

Pregnancy can be hard to detect in dogs, but after pregnancy has been diagnosed look out for the danger signal of vaginal discharge. Bloody discharge may warn of miscarriage, while a discharge of pus may be a sign of a womb infection. In both cases, contact the vet immediately.

Most bitches give birth without difficulty, but labour is nevertheless hazardous for a dog. If your dog is due to whelp, alert your vet, just in case he or she is needed. (See Chapter 6 for more information about whelping.)

emergencies and first aid

If you are in any doubt about your dog's health, contact your vet immediately. In the case of emergency situations, there are a number of ways of relieving your dog's pain and distress or administering first aid. You can treat less serious injuries yourself with first-aid measures before taking your dog to the vet.

First-aid Kit

Never mix up items in human and canine first-aid kits. Keep a separate kit for your dog and make sure that the vet's telephone number is included in it. You will need the following items:

I cotton batting
I cotton buds
I adhesive and gauze bandages in two widths, 2 and 4 in (5 and 10 cm)
I adhesive tape
I sharp-pointed scissors
I blunt-ended forceps
I a thermometer
I antiseptic cream and/or spray.

IF YOU SUSPECT YOUR DOG IS PREGNANT, ASK A VET TO CONFIRM IT.

IF IN DOUBT, ALWAYS CONSULT A VET.

Unconsciousness

If your dog collapses or becomes unconscious after an accident, you will need to check its airways, perhaps removing any foreign bodies and gently pulling its tongue forward to stop the dog's breathing from being obstructed.

Watch your dog's chest to observe its breathing – there should be between twenty and thirty breaths a minute. If exhaling seems forced, it may have an injured diaphragm.

Check its pulse on the inside of the hind leg, or press a hand on its chest, behind the elbow. Large dogs should have a pulse rate of between fifty and ninety beats per minute, and small dogs one of about a hundred and fifty beats per minute.

Do not spend too much time doing these things: an unconscious dog needs urgent veterinary treatment, so wrap it in a blanket and take it to the vet's.

Bleeding

If your dog is bleeding severely, it is an emergency. Try to control the bleeding while you are on the way to the veterinary surgery by applying a pressure bandage to the wound. (A tourniquet should not be used.) Place a large wad of cotton batting on the wound and bandage it firmly into place. If your dog is injured when you are not at home and have no access to a bandage, use whatever comes to hand, such as a scarf, sock, or T-shirt. The important thing is to slow the bleeding down.

Lighter wounds, which will probably stop bleeding within a short time, will probably only need to be cleaned with antiseptic. Trim the hair from around the wound to prevent it from becoming infected and watch out for any swelling, which would indicate an infection.

KEEP AN UNCONSCIOUS DOG WARM AND CALL A VET IMMEDIATELY.

A dog's skin does not readily bleed, and it is therefore easy to miss even deep cuts and scratches. A wound that is longer than about half an inch (a centimetre), or that appears to be quite deep, may need stitching. Unless it is bleeding profusely, do not attempt to administer any first aid and take your dog directly to the vet's.

If your dog has been injured in a traffic accident, or has suffered a serious fall, it may be bleeding internally. If it suddenly becomes pale and lethargic, alert the vet immediately.

Road Accidents

Many road accidents involving dogs can be prevented by ensuring that dogs are kept under control in urban areas.

A badly injured dog may be in shock and may bite you, so fit a muzzle using a lead, scarf, or rope before trying to examine it. If the dog is unconscious, try to put it on to a coat or blanket to make it easier to move it and avoid touching any visible injuries. Ask someone to help you to carry it to a car, using the coat or blanket as a stretcher, and take it to a vet's as quickly as possible.

If the dog appears to have a fractured leg, pick it up by supporting its chest under one arm and its hindquarters under the other, thereby allowing the affected limb to hang free.

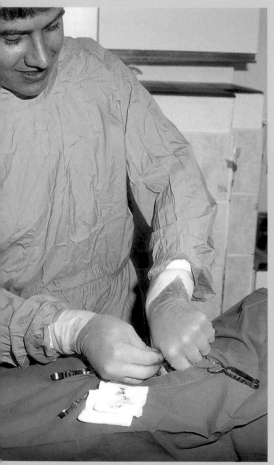

SERIOUS INJURIES REQUIRE VETERINARY HELP.

Bites

Unless the dog is bleeding profusely from a bite or has been really savaged, a bite is not an emergency situation. When dog bites take the form of puncture wounds they often become infected, so clean the wound with antiseptic and wait for twenty-four hours before deciding if you need to take your dog to see the vet, who will determine whether antibiotics are necessary.

Stings

Dogs are unlikely to die from insect stings unless the resultant swelling blocks the dog's airways or it has been subjected to multiple stings. Veterinary treatment is usually unnecessary unless the mouth or throat begin to swell. If it is visible, remove the sting with tweezers and apply a soothing cream or ice-pack to relieve the swelling.

Heat Exhaustion

Heat exhaustion is usually inflicted on dogs by careless owners, but some breeds, such as chows and bulldogs, are more susceptible to it than others. Never leave a dog in a vehicle without adequate ventilation and water: even on a cloudy day, the temperature can build up and heat exhaustion can kill a dog.

The signs of heat exhaustion are heavy panting, obvious distress, and an inability to breathe deeply. In severe cases, the tongue may appear swollen and blue. In such instances you must try to revive the dog immediately by bathing it in cold water, especially its head. Put it in a cold bath if possible, or a cattle trough if you happen to be near one, or drape a towel soaked in cold water over it. This really is life-saving treatment. Once it appears to be breathing more easily, take it to the vet's.

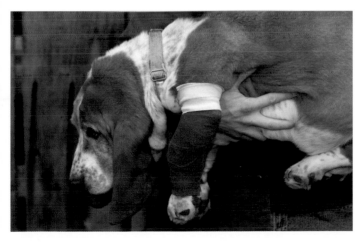

AN INJURED DOG WILL NEED CARRYING WITH CARE.

Poisoning

Dogs may either ingest poisons or suffer external contamination or burns from chemicals. If your dog has been in contact with caustic chemicals, sponge its coat with warm, soapy water. Do not use anything on your dog that you would not apply to your own skin, so do not, for example, use paint-stripper to clean paint from its coat, which is in any case highly toxic to dogs. Ask your vet for advice.

Internal poisoning can be fatal, so keep all toxic substances well out of your dog's reach. However, if it is clear that it has swallowed something untowards take it to the vet's immediately, preferably with a sample of whatever it has consumed, along with its packaging. Vomiting, diarrhea, fits, collapse, and coma are all signs of poisoning. If you know that the poison has been ingested within the past hour, try to induce vomiting by making your dog swallow a salt-water solution. Mix one teaspoon of salt with a cup of tepid water, administer the solution with a syringe, and stand by with newspaper or a bucket because vomiting will occur quite swiftly. Take your dog to the vet's as soon as possible, along with a sample of the vomit.

Common Poisons	Symptoms
Rat poisons are dangerous when consumed in great quantities. They are coloured to show their active ingredient, so take a sample or the packaging to the vet's to assist diagnosis.	Bleeding gums and bruising to the skin.
Household drugs: aspirins, tranquilizsers, or barbiturates.	Appetite loss, depression, staggering, coma.
Slug and snail bait (metaldehyde).	Tremors, salivation, fits, and coma.
Antifreeze.	Vomiting, staggering, convulsions, and coma.
Lead paint.	Vomiting, diarrhoea, stomach pain, and paralysis.
Household cleaners.	Inflamed skin, vomiting, diarrhoea, ulcerated tongue, and fits.
Toads: dogs may lick toads, some of whose skins are toxic.	Redness, swelling of the mouth and tongue.

Abcess: Swollen or inflamed area of body tissue, often filled with pus.

Acarus: A parasitic mite that can cause mange.

Action: The way a dog walks, trots, or runs.

Agalactia: Contagious viral disease that halts or slows milk production in a nursing bitch.

Agility trials: Competitive sport involving man and dog in which the handler directs his/her dog through a timed obstacle course; scoring is based on faults.

Albinism: Lack of pigmentation of the skin, hair, and irises of the eyes.

Almond eyes: Oval-shaped eyes that are pointed at either corner.

Alopecia: Unusual loss of hair, inherited skin problem that has no treatment or cure.

Alpha: The "top dog" of a pack.

Angulation: The angles of the bony structure at the joints, particularly of the shoulder with the upper arm (front angulation), or the angles at the stifle and the hock (rear angulation).

Apron: Ruffle of long hair on underside of neck and on chest of some breeds, e.g., Rough collies.

Back: That part of the top line of the dog between the withers and the pelvis. Length of back is not to be confused with length of body.

Bait: The tidbit or treat used to attract a dog's attention in the show ring.

Barrel: Ribs and body.

Bat ear: Erect ear, pointed at the top with a wider base.

Bench show: Dog show where dogs are displayed on benches except during ring sessions.

Bitch: A female dog.

Blaze: White line or marking extending from the top of the skull, between the eyes, and over the muzzle.

Blenheim: Chestnut and white colouring.

Bloom: Glossiness of coat.

Bobtail: A naturally tail-less dog, or a dog with a very short docked tail. The Old English sheepdog is often nicknamed "Bobtail."

Bordetella: Common respiratory infection; signs include cough, nasal discharge, and flu-like illness.

Breed standards: The physical makeup of breeds (colour, size, etc) agreed by national kennel clubs.

Brindle: A coat colour that is a mixture of black hairs with brown, grey, or tan.

Brisket: Front of chest between the forelegs.

Broken coat: Wire-haired coat.

Brood bitch: Female used for breeding.

Button ear: Ear that flaps forward.

Canine tooth: The long tooth next to the incisors in each side of each jaw; the fang.

Carpals: Wrist bones.

Castrate: Surgical removal of the gonads of either sex, usually said of the testes of the male (see neutering).

CEA: Abbreviation for collie eye anomaly.

CHD/HD: Abbreviation for canine hip dysplasia.

Chops: The pendulous upper lips or jowls of breeds such as bulldogs.

CPI: Abbreviation for canine parainfluenza.

CPV: Abbreviation for canine parvovirus.

Crabbing: Dog that moves with its body at an angle rather than straight ahead; also called sidewheeling or sidewinding.

Crossbreed: A dog whose parents are of different (but pure) breeds.

Croup: Portion of the back directly above the hind legs before the tail.

Dam: Female parent.

Dentition: The number, kind, form, and arrangement of the teeth.

Dew claws: Rudimentary toes on the inside of the metatarsus often removed shortly after birth.

Dewlap: Loose skin on the throat, e.g., bloodhounds.

DHLPP: Distemper, hepatitis, leptospirosis, parainfluenza, parvovirus vaccination.

Dish faced: A face with an upwards-pointing nasal bone.

Distemper (canine distemper virus): Often fatal, CDV. can cause vomiting, diarrhoea, pneumonia, and severe brain damage.

Docking: Surgically shortening the tail.

Dog: Any member of the canine family. Sometimes applied only to the male dog, the female being the bitch.

Drop-eared: Long, pendant ears.

Eye teeth: Upper canine teeth.

Fall: The hair that falls over the face of some breeds.

Feathering: Long hair along back of the legs or on the underside of the tail, e.g,. on setters.

Field trial: A competition for specific hound or sporting breeds. Dogs are judged on the ability and style of finding or retrieving game.

Flank: Sides of body between last rib and hip.

Flews: Pendulous upper lips that droop at the corner.

Front: The entire aspect of a dog, except the head, when seen from the front; the forehand.

Frontal bone: Skull bone over the eye.

Gait: The dog in motion, the way it moves as it walks or trots.

Gazehound: A sight hound.

Groups: Categories of dog recognized by national kennel clubs: sporting, hound, terrier, working, toy, non-sporting, and herding.

GSD: Abbreviation for German shepherd dog.

Guard hairs: The longer, smoother, stiffer hairs that grow through the undercoat to create the top coat.

Gundog: Dogs bred from hounds and herders, trained to retrieve game.

Haw: Inner lining of the eyelid, the "third eyelid."

Heat: Females' oestrus, the mating period for bitches.

Height: The vertical distance from withers to the ground.

Hip dysplasia: A hereditary condition in which there is excess laxity of the hip joint, eventually causing lameness and/or arthritic changes.

Hock: Tarsal bones that form the joint between knee and toes.

Hound: See scent hound and sight hound.

In-breeding: The mating of two closely related dogs.

Incisors: The teeth adapted for cutting; specifically, the six small front teeth in each jaw between the canines or fangs.

Jaws: The two bones that frame the mouth, holding the teeth.

KC: Kennel Club of Great Britain

Kennel cough: A contagious, usually mild, upper respiratory disease of dogs. Dogs in kennels or confined at dog shows are particularly susceptible, but there is a vaccination to help minimize the risk.

Leptospirosis: A bacterial infection that often leads to permanent kidney and liver damage.

Litter: The progeny of a bitch from a single pregnancy.

Liver: Deep reddish-brown colour.

Lyme disease: Illness transmitted by ticks that causes fever, arthritis, and lameness.

Merle: Blue-grey colouring with flecks of black.

Mongrel: Also known as random-bred: the product of parents of uncertain breed.

Muzzle: The part of the head on front of the eyes.

Nape: The junction of the base of the skull and the top of the neck.

Neutering: Removal of testicles from the scrotum.

Obediance trial: An event in which a dog and handler display their competence in executing specific skills such as sit, down, heel, and stay.

OES: abbreviation for Old English sheepdog.

Overshot jaw: Front upper teeth overlap, but do not touch the lower teeth. A fault in every breed.

Pad: Cushioned part of the foot.

Parainfluenza: A common respiratory infection in the dog. Signs include cough, nasal discharge, and flu-like illness.

Parvovirus (*canine parvovirus*): A potentially fatal intestinal viral disease causing severe vomiting and diarrhoea.

Pastern: Part of the leg below the knee in the rear legs.

Pedigree: Record of a dog's parentage.

Pointing: Stopping completely still on sight of game and pointing in that direction.

Purebred: A dog with parents of the same breed.

Quarters: The four regions that comprise a quadruped.

Rabies: A fatal infection affecting the central nervous system. The virus is transmitted primarily through the bite of an infected animal.

Rose ear: Small drop ear that folds over the back.

Scent hound: A hound that hunts primarily by scent.

Scissor bite: A bite in which the upper teeth overlap the lower teeth.

Season: The period of a bitch's heat or oestrus.

Second thigh: Area of the hind quarters between the hock and the stifle.

Setting: Stopping on sight of game and chasing it out once ordered.

Show dog: Dog bred for conformation to its breed standards and shown in competition on that basis.

Sickle tail: Tail carried extended and up in a semicircle.

Sight hound: A hound that hunts primarily by sight.

Sire: Male parent.

Spay: To render a bitch sterile by the surgical removal of her ovaries; to castrate a bitch.

Standard: An official description of the ideal of any variety.

Stifle: Upper joint of the rear legs that corresponds to a human knee.

Stop: Point between the dog's eyes.

Strip a coat: To remove dead, old hair from a wiry coat.

Stud: Male dog used for breeding.

Tail set: Position of the tail.

Topknot: Long, fluffy hair on crown of head.

Tricolour: Coat of three colours – black, white, and tan.

Undershot: Front teeth (incisors) of the lower jaw overlapping beyond the front teeth of the upper jaw when the mouth is closed, e.g., bulldog skull.

Vaccination: Immunization against communicable diseases.

Well let-down chest: A deep chest.

Well-sprung ribs: Rounded, rather than flattened, ribcage.

Wheaten: Coat of fawn or pale-yellow colour.

Whelp: To give birth to a litter of pups, used of all dogs and wolves.

Whelps: Unweaned puppies.

Withers: Highest point between the shoulder bones at the base of the neck; the point from which the height of a dog is usually measured.

Wry mouth: Lower jaw does not line up with upper jaw.

A

B

C

D

index

index

BIBLIOGRAPHY

Alderton, David, The Dog Care Manual, Quarto, 1986.

Bleby, John, and Bishop, Gerald, The Dog's Health from A to Z, David & Charles, 1986.

Cree, John, Your Dog – A Guide to Solving Behaviour Problems, Crowood Press, 1996.

Fogle, Dr. Bruce, RSPCA Complete Dog Care Manual, Dorling Kindersley, 1993.

Hamlyn Encyclopedia of the Dog, Octopus Publishing, 2000.

Johnson, Frank (ed.), The Mammoth Book of Dogs, Robinson Publishing, 1997.

Larkin, Dr. Peter, The Complete Guide to Dog Care, Lorenz Books, 1999.

Macdonald, David W. (ed.), The Complete Book of the Dog, Pelham Books, 1985.

Morris, Desmond, Illustrated Dogwatching, Ebury Press, 1996.

The New Encyclopedia of the Dog, Dorling Kindersley, 2000.

The Official RSPCA Pet Guide: Dog.

RSPCA Complete Dog Training Manual, Dorling Kindersley, 1994.

Stockman, Mike, The New Guide to Dog Breeds, Hermes House, 1998.

Woodhouse, Barbara, Dog Training My Way, Faber & Faber, 1955.

USEFUL WEBSITES

www.caninebehaviour.co.uk
www.k9web.com –
"Training Your Dog," Cindy Tittle Moore
www.insideout.co.uk
National Canine Defence League:
www.ncdl.org.uk
www.pawsacrossamerica.com
www.thepoop.com
www.un-reel.co.uk

ACKNOWLEDGEMENTS

The author and publishers would like to thank the following people for their assistance:
Photographic coordinator: Nick Juneman, A.M.B.I.P.D.T
Veterinary practice: McFarlane and Associates
Joli's Dog House
Cobham District Dog Training School
The Company of Animals
Assistant: Joanna Juneman